GU01607874

Taking Video Out of the Game

This book aims to provide information and in-routes to one of the most complex forms of video game accessibility. It promises to explain how a developer might make their game accessible to the totally blind. It will break down what that means and provide plenty of examples and ideas for how developers might achieve total blind accessibility, even in the largest, most complex games. As an experienced accessibility consultant who has worked on multiple AAA titles, the author brings a wealth of practical experience to the reader.

Brandon Cole was a totally blind, award-winning accessibility consultant working primarily in the video game industry. His notable work includes such titles as *The Last of Us Part I* and *The Last of Us Part II*, among others. He also used his social media, blog, and streaming platforms to advocate for accessibility whenever possible. Tragically, he passed away in June 2024 after a brief fight with Melanoma. You can still find his website, YouTube, and social media at brandoncole.net.

Taking Video Out of the Game

A Game Developer's Guide to Total Blind Accessibility

Brandon Cole

CRC Press
Taylor & Francis Group
Boca Raton London New York

CRC Press is an imprint of the
Taylor & Francis Group, an **informa** business

Designed cover image: Bret Cole

First edition published 2026
by CRC Press
2385 NW Executive Center Drive, Suite 320, Boca Raton FL 33431

and by CRC Press
4 Park Square, Milton Park, Abingdon, Oxon, OX14 4RN

CRC Press is an imprint of Taylor & Francis Group, LLC

© 2026 Brandon Cole

Reasonable efforts have been made to publish reliable data and information, but the author and publisher cannot assume responsibility for the validity of all materials or the consequences of their use. The authors and publishers have attempted to trace the copyright holders of all material reproduced in this publication and apologize to copyright holders if permission to publish in this form has not been obtained. If any copyright material has not been acknowledged please write and let us know so we may rectify in any future reprint.

Except as permitted under U.S. Copyright Law, no part of this book may be reprinted, reproduced, transmitted, or utilized in any form by any electronic, mechanical, or other means, now known or hereafter invented, including photocopying, microfilming, and recording, or in any information storage or retrieval system, without written permission from the publishers.

For permission to photocopy or use material electronically from this work, access www.copyright.com or contact the Copyright Clearance Center, Inc. (CCC), 222 Rosewood Drive, Danvers, MA 01923, 978-750-8400. For works that are not available on CCC please contact mpkbookspermissions@tandf.co.uk

Trademark notice: Product or corporate names may be trademarks or registered trademarks and are used only for identification and explanation without intent to infringe.

ISBN: 9781032560762 (hbk)
ISBN: 9781032557397 (pbk)
ISBN: 9781003433750 (ebk)

DOI: 10.1201/9781003433750

Typeset in Minion
by codeMantra

Dedicated in memory of Brandon Cole (1986–2024)

Dedication by Jackie Rudenick

Brandon has always been a remarkably intelligent child. As a single mother raising four children, I was often overwhelmed with responsibilities, but Brandon absorbed so much just by listening. He taught himself to play the piano and master video games at a young age.

Although I never fully grasped the intricacies of video gaming, Brandon's passion and talent in the field became evident as he grew older. He carved out a name for himself in the industry, showcasing his creativity and extensive knowledge. Despite my lack of understanding, I was always immensely proud of the recognition he received from friends and colleagues. Brandon's sense of humor and love for voice acting and school plays endeared him to many.

Late at night, Brandon and his stepdad, Mike, would often play video games together. When they heard the dog's bell, they would quickly jump into bed, thinking I was coming to scold them for staying up too late. It was only the dog, and we all shared a good laugh about it.

Brandon's friends were often baffled by his ability to beat them in video games despite being blind. Their frustration was endearing, and it highlighted Brandon's exceptional skills.

You will forever be in my heart.

– Love, Mom

IN MEMORY OF BRANDON COLE

For those who may not know, Brandon passed away before this book was published. I write this foreword to pay tribute to him and offer a glimpse into his life, aspirations, and achievements from a father's perspective. I was consistently in awe of his abilities, even at a young age—whether it was mastering the latest level of a video game, flawlessly imitating Sean Connery or Stewie Griffin from *Family Guy*, or simply being his amusing and quirky self. Brandon embraced his passion for video games when he received his first computer, a gift from *Make-A-Wish* that could engage with him, and he never looked back. He carried with him the dream of establishing a blog to assist the blind community in navigating video games and their accessibility as he moved from his home in Minneapolis to Ohio to be with his fiancée, Misty. He remained steadfast in this pursuit, taking on various jobs along the way, including providing customer service for tech support and lending his voice to characters in video games. His blog began to flourish, becoming a cornerstone for the blind community, and soon, game developers recognized his valuable insights, inviting him to speak at conventions. This led to his role as a consultant for games like The *Last of Us Part II, Forza Motorsport*, and several other major titles. This remarkable journey of passionately chasing his dreams enabled Brandon to forge a unique place within both the blind community and the video game industry, ultimately resulting in the honor of writing this book. Two poignant memories stand out to me: before he passed, he learned someone wished to meet him as their *Make-A-Wish* request, and I cherish the hours we spent as a child, playing *Diablo* and dreaming of him writing books while I illustrated the covers. One final dream realized. I am immensely proud of you, my son, and the man you have become. You will be deeply missed by many, and may your legacy endure.

Bret Cole

TO THE DEVS: A NOTE BY MISTY RAYBURN

Brandon loved his work, and he ultimately felt it was his path in life. Accessibility work was his element, and you'd never find someone more confident than he was when he was championing total blind accessibility. We saw it in his interviews, talks, and speeches. It was there in his live streams and his written work as well.

When asked, he'd give me credit for his start. He'd tell you that it was my idea for him to blog and that he showed doubt about it at first. While that's true, I witnessed his contagious excitement spread among developers in meeting rooms. I saw him grow from a gamer with ideas to a professional consultant who considered all options and all types of players, from the visually impaired to the totally new blind gamer who thought gaming wasn't an option for them. He even showed me that I wasn't just there for support, that I had an active role, and that my input as a consultant myself, with my own experience, was just as important.

Regardless, I still felt heaviness when Brandon told me if something should happen to him, and he lost his fight against cancer that he wanted me to continue his work. I said the same thing when he almost lost me to pulmonary embolism in 2017. We both knew this work was important. I still feel I have very big shoes to fill, but I hang on to him, telling me I was very important to the process.

He tells the reader a few times in this book that consultant input is important. I'm going to echo that. Needs change, technology changes, and it's hard enough to keep up with it all, let alone keep up with it and try to develop quality games. It takes a village to create accessibility. We're a network of accessibility leads at companies, champions, consultants, and players who love video games. We are all here at your fingertips and excited to help.

"The blind community is ready to work with you, and yeah that's basically it. We just want to play your games. We love you guys and uh I think that's the moral of my story."—Brandon Cole – GAconf 2017.

Contents

PART 2 Guidelines for Blind Accessibility in Games

Acknowledgments

THIS BOOK WOULD NOT exist without several people whom I want to acknowledge here. Firstly, my fiancée Misty, who kicked off my entire career with the words "You should blog," and whose love and support keep me going every day. She is the first pick on my team every time. And hey, from a blog to a book. Look at me now.

Secondly, Ian Hamilton, who not only agreed to be my official reviewer on this project but is responsible for plucking me from obscurity and placing me in front of the right people. I can never repay you for that.

Third, I'd like to thank my friends who have lifted me up throughout the years. Casey Kerian, who played so many games for me when I was young, and even years later, so I could experience them in some way. He's not the only one who has done this, but he has probably done it the most. Mike Breedlove, who continues to remind me of the power of my contribution to the world, and Victor Dima, who rallied behind me so strongly that I learned what it was like to have a superfan. Victor, I'm still waiting for that statue you promised. Also, Shay Baker, who made me start to feel important by agreeing to be my social media manager and is still the best one I've had. And to the many others who have sent me positive and uplifting messages and stories related to my work, I thank you all.

Of course, there's my fellow advocates and consultants. Steve Saylor, Morgan Baker, Paul Lane, James Rath, Carlos Vasquez, Josh Straub, Mila Pavlin, Emelia Schatz, and so, so many more. Thank you for being a part of this journey. All of us are working to make accessibility happen in our own ways, and I couldn't be more grateful.

I would also like to thank Danielle and my publishing team for taking a chance on an unpublished writer, trusting that we could still make something good and useful together. I appreciate that faith and hope, I have met that standard.

Lastly, a couple of nods to my own family. First, to my grandma Connie, who was probably the first to see greatness in me, way before I saw it in myself. Second, well, I have to thank my older brother Justin, whose prank kicked off a need for me to figure out and understand video games, and who therefore created the catalyst for what would become my career. And to my dad, who also played video games with me when I was young, but who, if all went according to plan, did some of the art for this very book. Pretty cool stuff, eh Dad?

Introduction

If you're reading this book, then you already know the awesome power of video games. They are a temporary escape from this world, gateways to places born from the deepest parts of our imaginations, and even a chance to be someone else for a while, which can mean a lot of different things to different people. For some, they're even therapy. Video games are an incredible medium offering a wide range of experiences. They can be art, they can tell amazing stories, or they can just offer you a way to pass the time. These experiences are extremely valuable, so when the question of why games should be made more accessible comes up, my first response is always "Why shouldn't they?"

Almost every developer I've ever met makes games because they want people to play them and to experience whatever it is their game offers to players. There is, therefore, very little point in thinking about that in a closed-minded way. Don't get me wrong, I don't think many game developers are actively doing this. Nobody's thinking, "I want tons of people to play my game, except for this group and that group." I think the real hurdle here is developers who haven't yet opened their minds to the possibility that the disabled COULD play their games if effort is given to accessibility. I've met some who still aren't aware that the disabled can play games at all, or that they want to. Trust me, they can, and they want to.

Of course, to open yourself up to the question of "Why not?" is to push aside all the arguments against the idea. Accessibility development might cost too much, the market might be too small to make it worthwhile, and so on. There are a lot of counterarguments to these, some of which we'll get into later, but here are a couple. While accessibility development will cost money, it will cost significantly less if it is begun earlier in the development process. Building accessibility as a core idea of your game will make it much easier for you to achieve. As for the market size, I daresay there are far more disabled gamers out there than you realize. According to the World Health Organization, an estimated 1.3 billion people experience significant disabilities. Making your game as accessible as you can to as many of them as you can will likely increase the game's market, possibly quite significantly. Plus, we're very, very loyal. That's a fact. Make your game accessible to the disabled, and we will stick by you just about forever. This is due to the fact that we don't have many options. We have games to play, but if you compare our availability of games to that of abled folks, the ratio is staggering.

The overall point here is that accessibility is the right answer. That is why I am writing this book. My hope is to reach those who want to implement blind accessibility into their games but aren't sure how. This book is your resource and should give you a solid starting point.

With that, let's get into it. There's a lot to cover here, and I sincerely hope you enjoy the ride. See you on the other side, and remember, the end of this book is only the beginning.

PART 1

The Story of Accessibility

CHAPTER 1

Defining Accessibility/ Inaccessibility

Accessibility is a far broader term than you might think. Part of the reason for this relates to perception. For example, many nondisabled folks think of the word accessibility as a synonym of approachability, which is a differentiation I often wish was clearer. The need to differentiate between those two things is actually the reason this chapter exists. I want to ensure that you head into the subsequent sections of this book with a clear understanding of what I mean when I talk about accessibility. To help us define what accessibility is, we're going to start with what it isn't.

When we say something is approachable, we often mean that it is easy to use or user-friendly in some way. The gaming industry typically refers to approachability as "pick up and play," which is fairly clear in its meaning despite the fact that it isn't a literal truth for some. If you are somewhat new to gaming, starting with something people consider approachable, or "pick up and play," may be the way to go for you. That, however, is a separate issue from accessibility.

So, then, what is inaccessibility? Well, the easiest way to answer is to say that inaccessibility is a lack of access, but what does that mean? To say something is inaccessible indicates that there is a barrier preventing access in some way. Something that prevents a person from using that app playing that game, getting up those stairs, reading that document, following that presentation, and a thousand more examples I could give is

DOI: 10.1201/9781003433750-2

an accessibility barrier. As a result, those things, the app, the game, those stairs, the document, and that presentation are all inaccessible to someone. And to be clear, when I say someone, I mean a whole group of people who share the same disability. The existence of even one of these barriers might mean the exclusion of a large number of people, which is of course what we are here to avoid.

This leads us to accessibility. To make something accessible is to smash those barriers. It's the wheelchair ramp that allows those with motor impairments to get up those stairs, the barrier is then smashed. It's the closed captioning that allows deaf people to enjoy that presentation, then that barrier is smashed. It's the full suite of blind accessibility features (navigational assist, traversal assist, narration, audio cues, aim assist, and so on) that allow the totally blind all over the world to complete The Last of Us Part I and Part II, barrier absolutely smashed. You get the idea. To make something truly accessible is to smash as many of those barriers as you possibly can. I'll be the first to tell you that it is difficult to make something that is accessible to absolutely everyone, but I encourage you to take it as far as you can and keep expanding on it in future projects. Trust me, those for whom your product is accessible will appreciate it immensely, and those for whom it isn't yet will appreciate knowing you're working on it. We'll talk more about this later. Consider that an early spoiler.

CHAPTER 2

Accidental Accessibility

The Tenacity of the Blind Gamer

Blind gamers have existed for many years, long before the recent, more blind-accessible games. In subsequent chapters, we will discuss some of the things that were made specifically for blind gamers back in the day, but first, I want to talk about the blind gamers who always wanted more. Those of us who just tried things, struggled mightily, figured things out, and sometimes succeeded at games that nobody thought we could, often including us. The passion with which we gamers pursue this hobby, the efforts we are willing to make in order to play a game we love. These are the things I'm going to show you in this chapter. It is a phenomenon I call blind gamer tenacity. I'm going to begin with a bit of personal history.

My entry into gaming came from a practical joke played upon me by my older brother. He convinced a 5 or 6-year-old version of me that we should go play Super Mario Brothers on our Nintendo, but handed me an unplugged controller while he played through the entire game. I was pressing buttons, but they were having no effect, and I had no idea until he delivered the punchline at the end. I was crushed at the time, to be sure, but I remember vowing that one day, I would beat one game without his help. Yes, at the time, it was only one.

So, I started trying games. The one thing the Super Mario experience taught me was that games had sounds that meant specific things, so the

DOI: 10.1201/9781003433750-3

experiment for me was to see whether I could use that information. Turns out, I could. I had limited success with many games, including Double Dragon, the WrestleMania game, Punch-Out, and more. I completely failed at other games, such as RoboCop, because there just wasn't enough audio information there for me to succeed. This was still an important step in the learning process, though, because each failure gave me an idea of what it was that these games were missing.

One fine day, I finally did beat a game without my brother's help. The game I beat was Killer Instinct for the Super Nintendo. This game had fantastic audio for the time. Each character has their own individual voice, which helped a ton. Also, the moves each character used were almost always unique in their audio composition. Sometimes, this was only because they were combined with the character's unique voice, but still, there was enough separation there that I could often identify which move was being used. This was important as I slowly learned the game's moves and combos, and finally beat it with Cinder, a fiery character with, admittedly, somewhat easy combos. Still, I never looked back. After the thrill of beating that one game, fulfilling that vow, I needed more.

So, I pushed forward, my gamer life having at last begun. I had a couple of other major successes, such as one particularly notable one with Metal Gear Solid for the Playstation 1. This was in a room that was crisscrossed with infrared beams. If broken, the doors slam, and the room is filled with poisonous gas that kills your character almost instantly. My stepfather was having trouble with this room, and on a hunch, I asked to give it a shot. He left the room, and I spent the next couple of hours, yes, hours, figuring out this one room. Through a combination of trial and error, and step-counting using the game's audio, I was able to determine when to move, how far to move at any one time, and when I should stand versus when I should crawl. All this data got me through the room. It took patience, but it was doable.

Another example I'll give here is Final Fantasy X. I played this game in its entirety, almost completely without any sighted assistance, save for two elements. The first was the Sphere Grid, Final Fantasy X's method of leveling up your characters. It used a series of nodes that you would have to move each character to in order to learn abilities or gain stats. All this was represented visually, and there was no narration for things like this back then, so I turned to the sighted and asked for help. The second element I needed assistance with was the game's required puzzles, known as the Cloister of Trials. These were puzzles that involved finding specific spheres and putting each in its correct slot. Other elements were often included, such as moving a pedestal into position, touching glyphs on walls, and in one case, utilizing a moving platform system. In short, with no navigational assistance of any kind, and no differentiation in the audio of each sphere, these puzzles were nearly impossible challenges without sight. Besides those two elements, though, I managed the game entirely on my own. There are environmental audio differences between areas, terrain differences for footsteps, reverb in some spots, different music, and so on, which helped with navigation somewhat. More importantly, though, navigation in Final Fantasy X is flat. I never had to worry about jumping onto a platform I couldn't see. I just had to be patient, and I'd always eventually find where I was supposed to go. All important dialog was also voiced, so I could use major characters as landmarks because they all said something if you clicked on them. Combat and inventory management were all menus, and menu memorization was a key component of blind accessibility back then, so I wasn't even intimidated by that. It felt natural to figure out each character's combat menu and even to relearn it again every time they got a new ability.

I wasn't the only one trying extremely hard to play video games, though. Others worked out methods for different games. As proud as I am of my Metal Gear Solid accomplishment (and I do still consider it a high point), I learned later that a blind person had managed to play the entire game. Some blind people would publish guides explaining what they figured out in certain games in order to help other blind people play them. This still happens today. I remember working on my own guide for a silly little game called Lifeline for the PlayStation 2. It was a game you controlled with your voice, and I had just enough help getting through it that I figured if people knew what to say at any given time, they could too. I never finished that guide.

The tale of blind gamer tenacity goes on and on. There are blind gamers who have done incredible things that even I cannot fathom. One regularly plays Call of Duty and has even reached a rather high rank. Keep in mind, though, that later Call of Duty games have incorporated some accessibility features; there are almost none for the blind. But that's not stopping this guy. Another has beaten the entire campaign of Diablo IV only days ago as of this writing, and though that game does possess some blind accessibility features, I can assure you this would still be no easy feat. Again, all of this has been to establish that we blind gamers love games like all other gamers do, and that we really, really want to play them.

Now, though, let's lean a bit further into accidental accessibility. I've already touched on it in some of the examples above, but essentially, accidental accessibility is when a game ends up being kind of accessible to us, even if it's not designed to be. Fighting games are the easiest examples of this, as they are the most accessible out-of-the-box genre. Most of them are 2D, meaning you never have to wonder about where your opponent is. They're always right across from you. In most modern fighting games, sound is positional, so we can use the stereo field to determine our position as well as our opponent's position on the screen. If our audio comes from the far left while our opponent's audio is on the far right, then it's safe to assume they're all the way across the screen, and we can start flinging fireballs.

There are other really great examples, though, such as the tremendous game 13 Sentinels: Aegis Rim. This game is part visual novel, part mech combat, and it's accessible for two reasons. First, it's simplistic navigation during the story bits of the game. Each area is laid out kind of like a side-scroller, with only occasional variation up or down, so we almost never get stuck moving around. Second, its use of small audio cues to indicate interactable objects or conversations, combat targets, and so on. These audio cues were likely just designed as little bits of UI flair, but they are absolutely an accessibility feature. Other things help too, such as the fact that all dialog is voiced, all audio during story moments is positional, and even your character's thoughts, which you can browse via a menu, are voiced by that character as you move over them. It's all pretty incredible, and 13 Sentinels is really a fantastic game.

The last example I'll give is one that inspired some of my own work later on. While Resident Evil 6 wasn't very well received by the Resident Evil community, it was very well received by the blind community due to its accidental accessibility features. The standout here is the PDA button. Pressing this button visually brings up the map on your character's PDA, with an arrow pointing at your next objective. More importantly, though, it also turns the camera to face that objective. The blind figured out that character movement followed the camera, and that you could just hold the PDA button while moving. The camera, and thus the character, would just keep on turning toward the objective as you moved this way, so using this feature, we could make our way (though much more slowly) to our next objective. The same principle worked when playing cooperatively, as holding down the co-op button keeps the camera locked on your partner, making it easy to follow them. These ideas later helped me, and the Naughty Dog team, brew up Nav Assist, which has now appeared in multiple games.

CHAPTER 3

Blind Accessibility Specifics

What It Means to Make Something Blind Accessible

It's time to focus on total blind accessibility specifically. While all accessibility is important, moving forward, we will strictly be discussing total blind accessibility. First, let's discuss its most basic idea.

Blind accessibility, when broken down, is all about information. Tons of information in a game, or any piece of content, is processed by the eyes, and that information is, of course, what we lack. So, when you first begin to consider making something blind accessible, you must consider that information and how to either provide it to us, or to work around its absence. Here are a couple of quick examples.

In film, TV, and now some video games, audio description provides us with some of those important visual aspects we would otherwise miss via a narration track overlaid onto the content. If you're unfamiliar with the way audio description works, then you should know there's an art to it. Audio description does not provide all visual information in an endless and constantly flowing stream. Instead, it is very carefully crafted to describe what needs to be understood in the moment and written in such a way that it doesn't step on any dialog or important sound effects. It is really

DOI: 10.1201/9781003433750-4

impressive to behold once you understand that. Anyway, this is all important to note because of things like context. While it's mostly obvious what information we're lacking because we cannot see it, we may be getting that information in some other way. Telling us a gunshot occurred after having told us a person aims their gun may not be necessary, depending on the circumstances. We know they fired, but it may still be important to tell us what was fired at. In any case, audio description is interesting because it is both a method of providing us with missing information and also a workaround because it cannot possibly tell us every single thing without much extraneous pausing.

On the gaming side, your basic visual novel can be made blind-accessible simply by adding screen narration features. The information we're missing in that case is just the text. Make that text read to us, and suddenly, the game is fully accessible. This only applies to a very basic visual novel, though, as many nowadays come with additional issues like the need to move a character around, even if briefly, or click on objects to locate something, or even play a mini-game of some kind to accomplish some task. But at its base level, a visual novel can be made fully accessible to the totally blind simply by narrating its text. We'll talk more about making specific genres blind accessible in part 2.

Let's go back to another non-gaming example and talk about images online. In their default form, they aren't accessible to us by their very nature, but that can be remedied with alternative text, also known as Alt Tagging, with descriptions of the image. Screen readers are built to detect and read these when they exist, so just providing those written descriptions can make image content accessible to us. It's also worth mentioning that even though some sites like Facebook attempt to generate an alt tag if one isn't present, they usually aren't particularly good. Some aren't terrible, but one written by you, since you know what information you're trying to convey, is always preferred.

I'll give two more examples, both of which are from The Last of Us. First, navigational assist, which is most definitely a workaround for missing information, as we are unable to see the environment around us. I deeply respect the art teams in the industry for the time and effort they put into their work, but no matter how much that is, that isn't likely to change for us. We'll just never see the environment around us. Some simpler games, and some audio games (more on those later too), have opted for navigational assistance in the form of sound cues that indicate walls, turns, objects, and so on, but making this work in a large 3D space may not be ideal, which is why the workaround here is the pathing The Last of Us uses both for navigating toward your objective or moving to scanned items or enemies in the area.

The next and last example I'll give here is the invisibility mode in The Last of Us. This mode is a huge workaround, and a bit of a concession. I fully admit I would've preferred to work on an accessible cover system. However, given the time and resources we had at the time, this was the best way to provide the blind with the stealth option, since we couldn't see areas where we could take cover. We worked hard to keep the challenge level customizable by providing a limited invisibility mode that scaled based on your stealth difficulty, but still, it is a great example of a workaround for missing visual information.

And so, like I said at the top of this chapter, information is the key. If you can figure out how to provide missing visual information, or give us the means to work around that missing information, you can and will make your game fully accessible to the totally blind.

CHAPTER 4

Accessible Beginnings

MUDs, Text Adventures, and So On

ONE OF THE FUN facts about blind game accessibility is that in the early days, we were playing many of the same games as everyone else. After all, starting in the late 1970s and lasting into the late 1980s and even early 1990s, one of the most popular types of game was entirely text-based. Even in the early 1970s, about 1971 in fact, there was a camera system developed by Opticon that allowed the blind to identify colors via a system of refreshable pins. This alone allowed them to play text-based games that utilized color to differentiate things, such as Lunar Lander.

It wasn't until the late 1970s, though, where text-based games were really kicked into high gear for the blind. Text-to-Speech systems began to be developed, such as a system called Votrax, which could be used on computers like the Vic-20. Thanks to pioneers of the text adventure genre like Scott Adams, who wrote Bespoke support for the Votrax system into many of his games, we could enjoy them on an equal playing field with the sighted.

Here's another little fun fact. While the Votrax system was an admittedly primitive speech synthesizer, it was actually used by the blind all the way through the 1990s, and even in the early 2000s. A device called the Braille 'N Speak, developed by Blazie Engineering, used the Votrax synthesizer presumably because of its low processing cost, and continued to do so through many, many iterations. The Braille 'N Speak and

DOI: 10.1201/9781003433750-5

devices like it were a specialized classification of device the blind referred to as a notetaker. These were essentially like palm pilots or PDA's for the blind. They used a six-dot braille keyboard, had a basic file system, and a few tools like a calendar and calculator. Eventually, there were games for this device too, though these were mostly very simple, short games as the device's capacity was very small. Still, back in my day, these were the go-to devices for schoolwork and leisure writing.

Let's rewind a bit from my school days back to the late 1980s, when more complex screen reader systems were built, such as Outspoken for the Mac, Vocalizer, and Jaws, which was developed in 1989 and is still going strong today. There were now more ways to access text adventures, and so we did. Then, the internet started becoming mainstream, and that introduced us to a brand-new type of text adventure: MUDs, which stands for Multi-user Dungeons.

MUDs were a kind of revolution for the blind. Now, not only could we type "open door," or "go north," and witness that action take place, we could do so with our friends online. Remember, for a time, MUDs were popular among many gamers, not just the blind, meaning that some of those friends were sighted. Eventually, though, many sighted gamers would move on from MUDs to more graphical interfaces for their multiplayer experiences. Those who once played MUDs would later play MMOs like EverQuest and Ultima Online. But for a long, long time, MUDs were the only answer to MMORPGs for the blind, as those more animated, less text-based games were quite inaccessible to us.

Believe it or not, there are still MUDs that persist in popularity today, such as Miriani, Alter Aeon, and the Discworld MUD. There are even modern apps that we can use to enjoy them, such as VIP MUD, which was created by a game developer known as GMA Games (more on them later), and MUDRammer, which is a mud client for IOS built with blind accessibility in mind. Some gamers even augment their MUD experience with sound packs, which, for the blind, is sort of the best of both worlds. Sound packs can be fairly complex in their construction, and so we can have both an interface that is easy for us to interact with, complete with descriptions of each room and zone that we can read, but also a seemingly full suite of sound effects and music. Footsteps, laser fire, individual combat sounds, and so on. There's nothing quite like a space battle in Miriani with a sound pack, let me tell you. It may not be as complex or work the same way as the big cinematic masterpieces of today, but there's something there to be sure! These were, and are, experiences that could achieve the same kind of intensity others were getting from games we couldn't enjoy, and I think that's why a few are still popular today.

I think now is as good a time as any to start talking about the Audyssey magazine. Started in 1996, the Audyssey magazine was an online publication distributed to interested blind gamers. It provided articles about accessible gaming and reviews of existing games that the blind could enjoy, some of which we will be discussing in future chapters. I truly believe the Audyssey magazine was responsible for many blind gamers expanding their horizons. While text-based games and MUDs were often discussed, Audyssey magazine also shed light on other types of games, including accidentally accessible games that existed back then, such as the original You Don't Know Jack and an interactive movie game called Silent Steel, and audio games. It made the blind interested and curious, made them want to branch out into different avenues for their gaming needs, and showed them that they could do so. Though it is no longer running, having been supplanted by other resources that now exist, I believe its impact on blind gamers cannot be understated. It certainly had an impact on me.

CHAPTER 5

Audio Games

GAMES FOR THE BLIND naturally progressed as blind gamers began to want more than text prompts. In the late 1990s and early 2000s, the age of audio games dawned. What is an audio game? It's a game in which the primary, and most of the time, the only channel of information was audio. This created some unique challenges, the resolutions to which inspired many of the blind accessibility features that exist in games today. Though many of these games were developed by the blind, we need to take a step back to get the full picture.

In 1974, Atari released a game called Touch Me. This was a simple audio pattern recognition game which was later imitated in other electronic games called Simon. For those unfamiliar, Simon was a game with four buttons, each of which played a note when pressed. The game would automatically play one note, then two, then three, and your job was to repeat the pattern using the buttons. While it was simple in mechanics, I promise you it could become quite challenging once you were trying to replicate patterns of ten or eleven notes. In any case, this was essentially the first audio game.

In 1997, while the audio games era was just beginning, a wonderful Japanese game developer named Kenji Ino decided to develop a game for the blind called Real Sound: Kaze No Regret. The game was originally developed for the Sega Saturn and was later released on the Dreamcast as well. This game was primarily a visual novel-style game, except with exclusively audio, wherein the player got to make choices that would determine how the story would proceed. It even came with a manual in braille. Even

DOI: 10.1201/9781003433750-6

more interesting, Kenji Ino convinced Sega to donate thousands of Sega Saturn consoles to blind people, along with the game, to ensure it would reach a market that may not have otherwise purchased the Saturn system anyway. It was a bold move, but it got the game in the hands of those it was intended for.

Now let's talk about some of the audio games the blind created themselves. There were many, many of these, so instead of mentioning them all, I will focus on a few innovative ones that set the bar and helped outline what a blind person would need in order to get experiences similar to those the sighted were getting from their games.

Super Liam was a game created entirely by an individual named Liam Erven, and is, as far as I know, the first ever side scroller for the blind. This was achieved through clever use of stereo panning. As you moved right through each stage, sounds indicating your next obstacle would fade in, whether that's an enemy, a hazard, or a powerup of some kind. First it would increase in volume, but then it would begin moving from right to center, the center position being your character's position. If it was an enemy, you could shoot it with your laser, and part of the challenge would be figuring out the laser's range and how much damage it did to each enemy. You could also just jump over it if you chose, though enemies would chase you a certain distance. Hazards, such as pits or the occasional ball of fire, would have to be jumped over. The edges of pits would be denoted by a couple of warning tiles before the drop, meaning your footstep sounds would change to be very specific footsteps denoting the oncoming danger. There were cut scenes, bosses, a scoring system, extra lives, multiple level types, and even secrets! It was a truly innovative game for its time.

Games like Alien Outback and Troopanum provided us with a Space Invaders-style experience wherein different types of ships would appear at different points of your stereo field, and you would move left or right, center them, then shoot them down. The positioning of each appearance was random, and this became quite challenging during later levels when ships were appearing nonstop. Some of them also had special properties, such as the ability to take multiple hits instead of one. These games were intense, wonderful, and very replayable experiences in some cases.

Shades of Doom is, very unashamedly, a Doom knockoff, but trust me, we were very OK with that at the time. Shades of Doom gave us the full shooter experience. We could navigate its levels using a compass key that told us the direction we were facing, turn indications in the form of audio cues for open spaces, audio cues for nearby doors and collectable objects, and a "visited" key, which would tell us, if pressed, if we had been in our exact position before, which was our equivalent of looking at the minimap to see which areas were filled in. It helped us not to get lost in some of the more sizable levels. Combat was handled with an audio targeting system. A constant beeping would indicate the system was active. When a target was nearby, the beep would increase in volume. Then, pitch would help you determine when you were facing your enemy dead on, and an additional sound added to the beep would indicate when the creature was in range and locked on for firing. The enemies were quite varied, and some were fairly interesting as well, such as one that would teleport you to a random spot on the map if it hit you. I hated that one.

A little game called Top Speed came up with an interesting idea for racing games for the blind which we will absolutely be discussing more in the second half of this book. The idea was a system using stereo panning to indicate the direction and steepness of the turn as it happened. There was a verbal cue as you approached each turn, but this allowed for greater immersion during the turn itself. The engine would pan in the opposite direction of the turn you were taking, as if retreating from you. Your goal was to pull your car back toward the center of your stereo field by turning in the correct way. It was an interesting and very effective approach, making races feel intense and dangerous at high speeds.

Monkey Business was a game that introduced us to the idea of true 3D movement, giving us the ability to turn in 360-degrees in a more open environment that wasn't primarily corridors. Shades of Doom allowed for 360 turning as well, it was just unnecessary except when precisely aiming. These were wider levels, like a beach or, in one case, an entire old west town. The story was fairly simplistic (monkeys escaped, go catch them), but it really was fun, and felt new at the time.

The same developer who brought us Monkey Business also gave us our first audio-only pinball game. The developer was ESP Softworks, and the game was ESP Pinball. The tables were all loaded with various audio sources, some of which were just points, but some gave you special bonuses or led to some kind of level completion, like any other pinball table. The concept that made the experience a bit more blind accessible revolved around the flippers. In ESP Pinball, the flippers were "sticky." When the pinball came in contact with them, it would stick there, and time would stop as an audio scan began. The scan would move over the table from the flipper to approximately 180 degrees away from it. As the scan proceeded, each point you could shoot for played a sound. Empty space was indicated by beeps, but individual audio cues were given to specific items on the table you might want to hit. If you were doing this scan on the Pac-Man table, for instance, you would hear a crunching sound as the scan passed over fruit. If you wanted to take a shot for one of these, you would press the appropriate flipper button when the scan was aiming at what you wanted, and the ball would shoot off the flipper in that direction. However, this was done in a semirealistic way. We quickly learned that it wasn't always wise to shoot straight for what you wanted. Sometimes there was a drain right in the way of the thing you wanted to hit, but we figured out that you could sometimes ricochet off of something else to hit your desired item. This, as I understand it, is a concept in regular pinball as well, the ability to learn tables over time and perfect your method of play on each one. ESP Pinball and its sequel, which was developed by a company now called Draconis Entertainment, were wonderfully fun games. Checkout Draconis, by the way. They're developing some fantastic things for the blind in the mobile and Mac spaces as of this writing.

Audio games today have come a long way. I suspect part of the reason for this is the ever-expanding accessibility conversation, but whatever the reason, more and more developers have become interested in making audio games. It's a genre that now goes well beyond blind developers, as several small indie teams have jumped on board, creating some incredible firsts. For example, a team called Somethin Else, which unfortunately has been disbanded, gave us the first audio-only games featuring well-known actors. Their game Nightjar, a short adventure about something gone wrong in a space station, featured the voice of Benedict Cumberbatch as someone trying to help your character make it through alive. Their game, Papa Sangre 2, about ghosts and spirits and the lord of the dead, featured Sean Bean as your primary antagonist, and he did an absolutely brilliant job. Both games were wonderful and of an extremely high quality, and it's a true shame we won't be getting more from this developer.

As is true with many games, some audio games inspired others. Games like Super Liam lead to the (among the blind), famous Bokurano Debouken series of incredible, lengthy, Japanese side-scrolling adventures. The specific bit of inspiration I want to talk about now, though, starts with a game called A Blind Legend. In this game, you either follow your guide (your character's daughter in most cases), using sound by turning to face her and moving forward, following her as she turns, or you fight. In combat, each arrow key or swipe, if you were playing the mobile version, would perform an action. Left would attack left, up would attack forward, right would attack right, and down would be your shield. The challenge was in the attack patterns of your enemy. Each enemy would attack in a different way, at different speeds, and so on. If they weren't attacking, though, they would be blocking, so you had to strike when there was an opening, putting yourself at risk based on your own knowledge of their patterns. If you wanted to play defensively, you could block them and strike immediately after a successful block, but if you didn't anticipate they would be using a combo attack, you could be headed for traded blows at best. It was a lot of fun when it originally arrived on the scene, and inspired what I think may be one of the best audio games to date.

The Vale: Shadow of the Crown is a tremendous audio-only adventure created by Falling Squirrel. In it, you are Alex, the blind daughter of a king who, due to tragic circumstances, must make your way over 500 dangerous miles to reach your home. Along the way, you meet several other characters, some of whom will help you and some who will not, you take on side quests, and you relive flashbacks of your younger years in your home kingdom. It's a really wonderful game with a great story, great sound design, and top-notch voice acting featuring several actors who have appeared in AAA titles.

Where am I going with this? Well, as it happens, The Vale's combat system is actually just a more refined version of that in A Blind Legend. The basic idea remains the same. Each enemy has its specific attack pattern and must be observed to be fought well. You strike when there's an opening but before you get hit, you can block and parry. Now, though, you can use a controller. The left thumbstick is your sword, the right is your shield because you can now block in different directions since you will also occasionally be facing multiple opponents at once, and whereas in A Blind Legend you blocked by holding the down arrow or swiping down, doing so in The Vale now charges up a power attack for bigger damage. However, now there's also stamina, which is a new factor you have to consider, and is communicated by the heaviness of your character's breathing. Oh, and there's also magic. Oh, and multiple weapon and armor types that affect all sorts of stats including your attack speed, how much damage you take when blocking, your ability to break an opponent's guard, and so on.

There are even multiple boss fights, each with its own mechanics. The whole thing is a blast, and I've played through it multiple times. Suddenly, I feel like playing it again!

As much as I personally love basically everything about The Vale, I think its biggest triumph is its marketing. If you're a completely sighted game developer sitting there reading this book, I would be willing to bet that you have at least heard of The Vale, even if by name only. This is because they did a tremendous job getting their game out there. They went to conventions, they developed an Xbox version, and have since been featured on Xbox's Games with Gold. For an audio game, that is tremendous exposure. The Vale is by far the audio game I have heard the most sighted people trying needs to stay the same because he is talking about people with vision trying a game that is pretty much audio only. I guess what I'm trying to say here is, "Hey, you should play The Vale."

There are a lot of great audio games out there nowadays. Enough that I could probably go on with this topic for some time. For now, though, I'll just mention a few more in the hopes you'll check them out. Blind Drive, (an arcade driving game), Alt-Frequencies, (a game wherein you can influence story events by interfering with radio broadcasts), Evidence #111, (an interactive audio drama where you can make choices that change the story outcome), and Stories of Blossom, (a point and click adventure game made for a younger audience, but played by older folks too because it is ridiculously adorable). Those are just a few suggestions, but I think they're good ones. Check out resources like audiogames.net for more, and enjoy what may be for you, the newfound world of audio games.

CHAPTER 6

Blind Accessibility's Mainstream Beginnings

IN EARLIER CHAPTERS, WE discussed the rise of text adventures and how the blind played as equals in that era. We also discussed Real Sound, Kaze No Regret, a Japanese game released for the blind on the Sega Saturn. Both of these are very early examples of the blind playing games in what you might call the mainstream, but now I want to discuss the beginnings of mainstream blind accessibility in the modern age. We'll still be going back a little, but not quite as far.

In 2008, a tiny little audio game called In the Pit, developed by R Hunter Gough, made its way onto Xbox Live Arcade. This was quite a significant event, much like The Vale penetrating the mainstream market was, as In the Pit is an audio game. You play a monster who lives in a pit underneath a king's throne room. When he is displeased with someone, he presses his secret button and sends them down through a trapdoor into the pit below, where you're waiting to greet them and eat them. The catch is that you, the monster, are blind, so you have to track them via their breathing and occasional voice lines. Their breathing gets louder as you get closer, and their heart beats through your controller at an increasing rate as you approach. Then, once you're close enough, you gobble them up with a press of the A button. The whole thing is played for laughs. There are no gruesome sounds here. Still, aside from a few victims with abilities that help them while in the pit and give the game a little bit of challenge, that's essentially

DOI: 10.1201/9781003433750-7

it. It's a simple game, but had a great impact on me, and probably many of the blind gaming community at the time.

I had an Xbox 360 when In the Pit was released because, well, of course I did. I was a gamer through and through, and I utilized accidental accessibility to the fullest, and wouldn't hesitate to just mess around with stuff either. But this was a first. A game essentially made for me and others like me was available on the same online store as all these other games people were playing. That meant a lot to me, and I still think of In the Pit to this day.

I want to provide some additional perspective here. While researching for this book, I came across a video review for In the Pit done by a Youtuber who goes by @CGRUndertow. This reviewer made an interesting comment near the end of their review that, having read the previous chapters in this book, will likely interest you more now than it would have. They said that a few games had tried this "kind of blind gameplay," but "few if any have done so this successfully." Think about that comment for a second. Think about where that comes from. I do not judge the reviewer in any way for making it, because it comes from their perspective as a sighted gamer. This was 2008. Tons and tons and tons of audio games had been created by this point, so for us blind gamers, the draw was just that it was on Xbox, not that there were no other games providing us with this kind of experience. But for CGRUndertow, this was something completely new. Something that fell outside their understanding of what a game could be. I can appreciate that, and I take no issue with that. I just think looking at things from new perspectives, especially after you've gained certain knowledge, is interesting, and helps to bring it all together.

Let's fast forward to 2009. This was the year VoiceOver launched for the iPhone. VoiceOver is a screen reader that changes the way iPhone touch gestures work in order to make touch screens accessible to the blind. The most basic description of how this works is that we have two navigational choices. With VoiceOver active, we can swipe left and right in order to snap between on-screen elements, and double tap with one finger when we're on the element we want. Swiping right will always move to the next button, or link, or text area, and swiping left always moves to the previous. Also, it doesn't matter where we physically double tap, as the VoiceOver cursor, (basically the memory of the last element we moved to), will remain on that element unless we change it. Alternatively, we can place a finger on screen, move it around, and hear elements as our finger is on top of them, then lift it when we find the one we want the VoiceOver cursor to land on, and double tap anywhere to select. This latter method gives us a better understanding of where elements are physically located on screen.

I'm telling you all this because I want you to have a basic understanding of how this worked in order to understand the impact it had on us. VoiceOver launching on the iPhone, and Apple supporting VoiceOver within all their apps, and in such a way that many other apps didn't even have to be modified to support it, flung the floodgates wide open. Suddenly, we were as connected as our sighted counterparts were. Suddenly, we could use many of the same apps as they could. Before this, our cell phones may have had something resembling a screen reader, but usually they could only do a couple select things, like make calls and send texts, with very, very occasional support for some other apps. Now, there was an almost overwhelming number of things we could access, and yes, this included games.

The earliest games we could access were those that already used standard iOS coding conventions. These were natively supported by VoiceOver, and so didn't have to be modified in order to be enjoyed by us. I remember playing a lot of the Storm8 games back then. The kinds of games where you had a certain level of energy you could spend in a given hour, and they were mostly all the same with slight differences between each. I remember playing Hanging with Friends, which the developer was apparently shocked to learn was blind accessible. Those are just a couple of examples. But things really picked up when mobile developers got wind that we wanted to play their games and started working to intentionally implement blind accessibility.

I've already mentioned the developer Somethin Else in the audio games chapter, but their efforts were a direct result of the huge adoption of iPhones by the blind. Remember how the iPhone got VoiceOver in 2009? Well, their first game, Papa Sangre, came out in 2010. They were quick, and we loved them for it. I remember feeling surprised at the quality of some of the early mobile games like Papa Sangre and Soul Trapper. Their audio design was fantastic, their voice acting was top notch. I felt almost welcome in the mobile gaming space, even though the ratio of games we could play to games we could not was and is still massive.

In 2013, we saw mobile developers not only adding blind accessibility to their games but tracking usage data of blind accessibility features. One game, called Solara, was able to determine that, following the addition of VoiceOver support, the blind community became their most loyal players, and spent the most money on the game. Another developer, who made a mobile MUD client called MUDRammer and later added accessibility support in a single day, quickly found that 10% of his user base were using screen readers, and that figure rose to 16% shortly after. The moral of this story, game devs, is that accessibility breeds loyalty. Remember that one. Make the effort for accessibility, and we will reward you with our undying gratitude.

As more and more games and apps flowed onto the IOS app store, the blind community cooked up a site called AppleVis to discuss which apps were and were not accessible and review various apps and games to point the blind to those they could effectively use. It is still an invaluable tool today, and here's an even cooler fun fact. As of this writing, AppleVis data shows over 400 blind accessible iOS games. I definitely recommend them as a resource to mobile game developers, as their reviews are broken down by specific accessibility needs. An example of this is whether or not all buttons in an app are labeled properly. A game in which this is not true might still be playable, but we appreciate the removal of that extra frustration of figuring out what an unlabeled button does.

Going back again to 2009, Stevie Wonder made some waves, as he was asked to present the best music game at the Grammy Awards and took the opportunity to use that platform to promote accessibility. His speech got huge cheers, and while some of those cheers may have been because, well, it's Stevie Wonder, I believe that somebody somewhere was influenced that day. It was one of the biggest calls for accessibility on one of the biggest televised platforms. Millions would have seen it. I think it's more than deserving of a mention here.

Jumping forward again to 2010, we have the signing of the Twenty-First Century Communications and Video Accessibility Act (CVAA) by U.S. President Obama which, in short, made it law that devices that supported any kind of communication had to be made accessible enough that a disabled person could use its communication functionality. At the time, a waver was given to the gaming industry, but as of 2019, that waver no longer applies. Still, the significance of this moment can be seen even before 2019. The existence of the CVAA prompted console makers to act. Text to speech was introduced to PS4 for the first time ever, supporting only basic functionality at first but improving drastically over time, and eventually leading to the PS5's system-wide screen reader. Nintendo has notably not followed this trend just yet, but they have at least started down the road of considering some accessibility features, so there is still a little hope for the future.

Now we get to 2013, where one blind man's skill resulted in an accessibility shift. Carlos H Vasquez, a totally blind gamer who happens to be extremely skilled at fighting games like Mortal Kombat, managed to make it to Evo, an annual world-wide fighting game tournament, as a participant. There, he got to show off his skills, and NetherRealm Studios, the creators of games like Mortal Kombat and Injustice, took note. They approached him and asked him what he would need for their games to be more accessible. Carlos explained the idea of audio cues to them, and they were interested. Off they went, and before long, a feature was added to Injustice: Gods Among Us. Suddenly, you could turn on an audio notification for when your character, or your opponent's character, was in range to interact with an environmental interactable. These were objects in each stage that could be used for doing damage or sometimes just getting quickly across the screen. They were significant enough that they could turn the tide of a match and were thus very important. The addition of this audio cue, which gave blind players information they were missing before, simply made us better at Injustice and, since NetherRealm chose to bring the environmental interactables forward, their future games as well.

In 2014, a developer working on another fighting game called Skullgirls decided he wanted to help out its blind players as well. With minimal consultation, and a couple days work using a library called Tolk, he was able to add full screen reader support to the game. This meant that the game did not have native narration, but if the user was running a screen reader, this would be detected, and all text output would be sent to it. This was massively successful, as it opened up parts of the game that were previously difficult to work through, such as tutorials and, at the time, the text of the game's story mode. We could also read menus, including character move lists, enabling us to do a lot more practice within the game instead of having to look up lists others had posted online. So much functionality was created for us just because screen reader support was added. Remember that fighting games are generally fairly accessible out of the box, and this was no exception. This was the last piece we needed to fully enjoy this great game.

In 2017, a developer called PopCap Games noticed how inaccessible games made in Unity were for blind people. This is because Unity typically uses nonstandard controls, sending everything to your screen as a video image that can be interacted with. However, since even in-game text was part of these images, screen readers like VoiceOver could detect nothing at all in a Unity Game. To us, games made in Unity were blank, noninteractable screens. PopCap Games decided to do something about this and designed an incredible Unity accessibility plugin that mimics the behavior of VoiceOver within Unity. VoiceOver still technically wasn't functioning when playing a game with this plugin, but their version of it was, and it worked just about as well. The first use of this plugin was in PopCap's own game, called Crafting Kingdom, which is still played by many blind people today. It has since been used by multiple other developers to create accessible experiences in Unity and now even works on PC games.

CHAPTER 7

AAA Accessibility Reaches the Totally Blind

I WON'T LIE TO YOU. This chapter is going to be pretty unashamedly about The Last of Us Part II, the first fully blind accessible AAA game, released in June of 2020. The Last of Us Part II was a turning point in the understanding of blind accessibility and game accessibility in general, and I was honored to have been a part of making that happen. In this chapter, we'll discuss how this was achieved and break down some of the features that made TLOU2 stand out for the blind.

Accessibility was a part of the thought process from the beginning for Naughty Dog, the developer of The Last of Us Part II. They wanted to go all in with it, too, which is exactly what they did. Early on, they set a very good precedent by hiring not just one or two, but a total of seven accessibility consultants with different specialties in order to help them make TLOU2 as accessible as possible. I was hired on as the blindness accessibility consultant, Steve Saylor and James Rath were the low vision consultants, Morgan Baker was the deaf/hard of hearing consultant, Paul Lane and Josh Straub consulted on motor-impairment accessibility, and Ian Hamilton was brought in as a general accessibility authority. Pro tip, game devs, follow all of these people. All of them can provide incredible insights which could help you achieve multiple kinds of accessibility on

DOI: 10.1201/9781003433750-8

your projects. Ian Hamilton was a major source for this very book, as he is a master of collecting accessibility-related data, among other things. Trust me, you won't regret it.

The idea of how blind accessibility would be achieved was, in my opinion, based on the reactions I observed, a scary one for the folks at the studio. However, one of the key factors is that each and every one of those folks was willing to listen and take in the information that would eventually lead us down the right path. Some of my favorite moments during this process happened in our brainstorming sessions, where we were just throwing out big ideas and discussing what was possible. I learned a lot during this project, and much of it happened there. We had our doubters, though, which is understandable, considering nothing on this scale had been attempted before. A few folks weren't sure if what we were proposing could be done at all. To be honest, it was those stories that ultimately made me the happiest coming out of that studio. The moment when they not only realized that we could do this, but that we should do it, and they fully committed. I loved that.

Another aspect of this that should be discussed is that everyone in the studio got involved. I was told near the end of the project that there wasn't one person who hadn't touched accessibility in some way. Of course, this would include all types of accessibility, not just blind accessibility, but it's something I loved to hear. This was a studio-wide effort, and yes, to guarantee the best experience, that's how accessibility should be approached. It should be viewed as a part of development just as important as any other. I loved just how many groups of people wanted my input. I had plenty of meetings about gameplay, of course, but I also had meetings with audio, design, and even UI. My input on the layout of the accessibility menu in the options screen was considered important, and that felt pretty good. To make something truly accessible, it had to be equally accessible across the entire experience, which is something Naughty Dog understands.

Let's break down some of the individual features that made TLOU the experience it was for the blind. We'll talk about this kind of thing more in the second half of this book, but for now, we'll discuss them as they specifically relate to this game. First is narration. While The Last of Us Part II does not use a Text to Speech (TTS) engine for its narration, opting instead to use individually recorded files to achieve the same result, it stands out because every single thing is narrated. All of the remappable controls, every menu item and its associated tooltip, every in-game tutorial message and tooltip, the crafting and upgrade menus, photo mode, and, of course, all the little in-game lore notes you can find along the way. Everything presented to a sighted player as text is narrated by this game if the feature is enabled. Believe it or not, that was fairly uncommon back then. There are more and more examples of this these days, but in 2020, this was revolutionary. On top of that, narration was available in every supported game language as well. We tried our best to leave nobody behind.

The next thing that really set the bar was the navigational assist features, which included both the navigational assistance and the Enhanced Listen Mode. Based on a bit of accidental accessibility from Resident Evil 6, which allowed you to walk to your objective simply by holding the map button, our nav assist cast out a ray in the direction you needed to go on the press of a button and turned the camera that way as well. Once you reached the point where that ray was cast to, you would be notified via an audio cue and press the button again to cast the next ray. The markup for each of these tiny waypoints was done by hand, which is something I truly admire. The point is this would eventually lead you toward your objective. The second half of this, the Enhanced Listen Mode, would allow you to scan for nearby items or enemies and path find toward one or the other if you chose. This would allow the blind to move in on their enemies, either to get in range for a shot or for a stealth takedown, and scanning for items allowed them to loot the many, many items hidden throughout the game. Together, these features were what made it possible for the blind to successfully traverse the 30-hour story of the game, a truly monumental accomplishment.

Next up, the many audio cues we used to convey information in the game, as well as the audio glossary, an idea taken from audio games that had been doing it for years. The audio glossary provided a comprehensive list of all the audio cues a player might hear during gameplay, as well as a way to play them and thus get an example, and tooltips that describe the situations in which you might hear that particular sound. Best of all, this audio glossary can be accessed at any time, either before you start playing, or at any point during the game via the pause menu. With the sheer number of audio cues that exist in the game, cues for when to jump, when to crouch, when to interact, when to dodge an attack, when to use a melee attack and many, many more, this glossary was an essential feature, and needed to be easily accessible, since blind players would need to be able to familiarize themselves with them as much as they wanted. These audio cues are a critical source of information, as well as a method of providing different information through different channels, rather than trying to funnel everything through TTS (text to speech).

Next up, I want to discuss The Last of Us Part II's Invisibility while prone feature. This is a feature that does exactly as advertised. It makes you invisible to enemies while your character is prone. This feature is important to this discussion because it highlights the difficult balance between preserving the sighted user's experience and providing functionality for the blind. It is a feature I wrestled with, as I wanted to ensure we weren't simply making the game too easy, as that is never my goal. One of the toughest concepts you'll have to work through in this book, however, is this. While a feature like invisible while prone, or many of the other accessibility features, might make the game easier for you, it merely levels the playing field for someone who is disabled. That is why this balance is difficult, and one of the reasons consultants will forever be an important step in this process. I do want to break this down a bit further though.

First, the concession. We built this feature because we wanted to ensure the blind had access to stealth gameplay. The sighted would constantly get the choice of whether to approach encounters quietly or go in guns blazing. That choice should be available to the blind as well. However, even I didn't think that being invisible while prone was the perfect solution. Ideally, I would've wanted to be able to utilize cover that already exists in the game to avoid being spotted. There are ways this could've been done, such as audio cues to denote possible cover points or a point-to-point system such as the one in Gears of War. However, given all the other features that were being worked on, some of which like narration and nav assist being particularly complex, not to mention the sheer number of features being added for accessibility, we didn't have the resources necessary to build that kind of system. So, this was a concession, but one that was carefully thought through.

Second, the confession. When I first tested the invisible while prone feature, I thought it was too easy. I acknowledged its usefulness in providing stealth gameplay to the blind, but it felt like a bit too much. Those discussions led to a couple of changes. First, we decided that, should an enemy do the equivalent of stepping directly on your prone character, that would count as detection, and you would be spotted. Second, the absolutely brilliant "Limited Mode" was introduced. When activated, your invisibility was limited by time, and how much time you had was determined by the stealth difficulty you had chosen. At the highest stealth difficulty level, your invisibility lasted for only 6 seconds or so. I thought this was a fantastic workaround because it fit in with the game's entire philosophy of customizable difficulty.

There are more accessibility features I didn't cover here, such as traversal assistance, dynamic aim assist, and more. I could probably discuss The Last of Us Part II for pages and pages, but I think the points have been made. The Last of Us Part II was an absolutely huge turning point in blind-accessible gaming. It rocketed us into the AAA space and welcomed us there. It created hope in some blind gamers where little to no hope had existed. It even sold consoles, as some purchased PS4's JUST to play this one revolutionary game. The stories I've heard of blind people who thought gaming just wasn't an option for them until they found this game still warms my heart, and I still occasionally receive new thank you messages for my work on this game. What we did on The Last of Us Part II is something I will carry with me forever.

CHAPTER 8

The State of Blind Accessibility

If you're just getting started with all this blind accessibility talk, if this book has been your gateway to it, you may be pleased to hear that blind gaming accessibility is in a pretty good place right now. Make no mistake, we have a long way to go. We are far from my ideal world, where most games are accessible to us, but things are headed in a generally positive direction. In this chapter, we'll outline some of the things that are happening and some recent innovations to give you some idea of where we currently stand.

In the previous chapter, we talked a lot about The Last of Us Part II. That game inspired accessibility features in many others. In the AAA space, it inspired many of the blind accessibility features that appeared in God of War: Ragnarok. Nav assist was there, though it worked quite differently from The Last of Us Part II's version. Narration was present, and it worked the same way The Last of Us Part II's narration worked, though it was not as complete, missing in a few important areas such as the shop and upgrade screens. Audio cues were also present and, because both games were made by Sony studios, resources were shared. The audio cues were actually the same, familiar audio cues players were already used to hearing from their time with The Last of Us Part II, with the exception of new audio cues that were created to fill gaps for things The Last of Us Part II didn't have. TLOU2 didn't need, for instance, an audio cue indicating

DOI: 10.1201/9781003433750-9

when to throw your axe, or fire a particular type of magic arrow at a target. These things would've been interesting in that game for sure, but no, we'll leave the ice axes and sonic arrows to God of War.

The Last of Us Part II also inspired accessibility in the indie gaming space. A game called 1428, Shadows Over Silesia contains features that are heavily inspired by those in TLOU2. In some cases, such as navigational assist, these features are improved upon, allowing you to be specific about what you're navigating to, rather than just letting you choose the closest item, the closest enemy, or the golden path. There's even a feature that gives you a description of the current screen you're on. Puzzles have also been modified in a way I approve of, meaning they're still puzzles, but modified just enough to be accessible to the blind if certain accessibility features are enabled. It's a challenging and lengthy action adventure that did some wonderful, innovative things with accessibility, building on what had come before it.

Naughty Dog also built on what they had made when they released The Last of Us Part I, a remake of the original game. This remake incorporated all the accessibility features from The Last of Us Part II and went on to make them better. One small but powerful improvement was with nav assist, which now brought you to a safe if you found it, didn't crack it, then found its combination. Perhaps I should explain this a little more.

Firstly, in TLOU2, there's a system in place which you can use to crack a locked safe using audio. It's one of the most awesome accessible by design features I've encountered. Just by listening for slightly different clicks as you turn the combination dial, you can get into those locked safes without having to find the note or the sign that gives you the combination. This feature became sort of essential for the blind because of a flaw in the way enhanced listen mode worked with nav assist. As I mentioned, the way it was implemented, you can only path find to the nearest item to you based on your enhanced listen mode scan. Once you find that item, it disappears from the scan, which makes sense in most cases. This includes safes, though, because if it didn't, you'd just be stuck there until you opened it, and couldn't get any other items without some fiddling to make something else closer to you than the safe is. So, safes and workbenches disappear from the scan as soon as you find them, regardless of whether you finish with them. The problem is that, if you then left, thinking "OK, gotta find the combination," and then found it, you couldn't get back to the safe, because as far as the scan was concerned, it's gone. The remake fixed this issue for TLOU1, as it temporarily rerouted the golden path to a safe if you found the combination and it wasn't yet unlocked. To be clear, this was still a band-aid solution, as I would've preferred nav assist allow for some player selection, but it solved a long-existing problem, so I was OK with it.

TLOU1 was innovative in another way, too. It also contained audio description for its cinematics and was the first game to do so. It definitely wouldn't be the last, though. Anyway, to give you the basics here, audio description is a narration track that describes visually conveyed information to a blind person. It is widely used in movies and TV these days, and many streaming service providers have adopted it. Those who write audio descriptions are professionally trained to be concise, yet informative, focusing on not stepping on any dialog or important sound effects while describing a scene. Including this feature in TLOU1 opened up a lot more information to the blind. They now knew things they never had before, though this wasn't quite as complete as I would've liked. The restriction to the game's cinematics was heftier than it might sound, since so many of the game's cut scenes are done in-engine. Whole swaths of noninteractive moments are undescribed, such as the car trip at the beginning of the game. Still, this was the first implementation of audio description in a game, and for what was done, I am still quite happy with it.

Now, while still not common, audio description is becoming much more widely used in games. Games like Stories of Blossom, an adorable point-and-click adventure game which is audio described the whole way through, Mortal Kombat 1, Stray Gods, Forza Motorsport, and more feature brand new innovations in the area of in-game audio description. For example, Forza has dynamic, in-game audio description based on time of day, weather, and so on, and description happens even in certain gameplay moments, such as driving into the pit. Audio Description is just another way to help immerse the blind in your game's world, and if it's not already part of your plans, I would recommend making it one. When you do, check out a professional audio description company called Descriptive Video Works, and tell them I sent you.

Lots of other games have been getting attention in the blind accessibility space for other reasons as well. Games like As Dusk Falls, which was fully blind accessible at launch thanks to some incredible narration work (basically all it needed as an interactive cinematic experience), gave us a tense and wonderful story about family and how it can be impacted by stressful situations. Sequence Storm, which had blind accessibility patched in over the course of a summer and is now fully blind accessible, gave us a fascinating and fun rhythm and racing hybrid. Speaking of hybrids, Brok the InvestiGator, which also patched in blind accessibility post-launch, gave us an extremely long, extremely fun point and click adventure/Beat ‘em up hybrid. Games like Blind Drive, Alt Frequencies, The Vale, Apotheorasiss, Evidence #111, and more continue to give us ideas of what an audio game can be. There are many, many more games out now that we can play, and it’s not nearly as infrequent as it used to be to see a new one emerge. I’ll reiterate that our list is still small compared to the amount of games that come out nearly every day, but it’s wonderful to watch it get larger.

I also want to give a nod to the studios that are making steady progress toward blind accessibility. Studios like Ubisoft, for example, whose games have year over year reached steadily toward that goal. They’re still not blind accessible, but something new is typically added with each release. They’ve reached a level now where their screen narration is pretty solid and nearly complete in their games, and Assassin’s Creed: Valhalla even had audio cues to help locate items. It’s a long process, but they’re getting there. It is quite difficult to dive all the way in the way Naughty Dog did, and I appreciate that.

Ubisoft aren’t the only one, though. Studios like Insomniac Games have begun perfecting their accessibility craft. Many of their newer games feature tons of accessibility features, some of which do help the blind, but none of which yet make their games fully accessible to us. I like to talk about the Spiderman 2018 remaster and Miles Morales when I talk about Insomniac, because in my opinion, those two games are so close to accessible that it hurts. They do lack screen narration, but they have a nav assist that is semi-functional. The problem is that it’s a simple implementation that uses only the camera position rather than smart scripting, but it almost, almost works in those games because most of the time you’re swinging through the city, so navigating as the crow flies is legitimately a decent way of doing things. It all breaks down, though, when you’re on the ground and are expected to find your way through some building or warehouse or huge enemy compound. You get the idea. Since there is no scripting to guide us around things, it attempts to send us into walls constantly while saying “Yeah, seriously just go that way. The thing you want is right through there!” But let me tell you, completing the intro to Marvel’s Spiderman: Miles Morales, which takes place in the open city, thrilled me intensely, which is why

I say that it hurts. The feeling of being brought down by the realization of what was happening, why the few things that worked were working for a while. That is painful. The realization that I would not be playing that game to completion, despite my soaring hopes that I might be. That is painful. Insomniac is so close, it hurts. But maybe, just maybe, by the time this book is in your hands, this will have already changed.

Several studios started with narration when approaching the idea of blind accessibility, and that is OK as long as improvements are made afterward. A couple of great examples here are Gotham Knights, which, from what I can tell, has basically perfect narration but just about nothing else in terms of total blind accessibility, and Hogwarts Legacy, which also has incredible narration despite not having much else for us. I do often refer to narration as step one, as it is the blind accessibility feature that will universally be needed for almost every game, so I'm glad these studios are beginning to bring it in. Still, of course, I always want more.

All these accessible games are of course wonderful, but the state of blind accessibility goes beyond the games themselves. At last, we're beginning to see true engine support for blind accessibility features. While Unreal began experimenting with accessibility some time ago, adding color blindness features in 2014, they have more recently added screen reader support to their engine. The earliest example of this is 2019's Halo: The Master Chief Collection, but it has since expanded into the mobile space. Games like Mortal Kombat Mobile and Injustice Mobile, both support IOS's VoiceOver thanks to the work Unreal did. Apple has also announced their very own accessibility plugin for the Unity engine, making blind accessibility far easier by allowing you to add VoiceOver labels to those custom Unity elements. These are two of the biggest engines in use for game development today, so this can only mean good things for us. Not to mention those studios that have already done tremendous accessibility work are making accessibility a part of their custom engines, so their process for making a game blind accessible will be even easier going forward. All this means is that I need more games, and I'm very OK with that.

This is where we currently stand with blind game accessibility. I think you'll agree that we're in a pretty good spot, but like I keep saying, there's always room for more. There is still so much uncovered ground, but now it's time to start covering it. So far in this book

I've attempted to help you understand the basics of blind accessibility, how it has been done before, what is happening now, and through all that, why you should pursue it. Now, at last, it's time to get into the question of how. Now, it's time for me to help you take your first steps toward blind accessibility in your upcoming projects, whatever they may be. Read on because we're just getting started.

PART 2

Guidelines for Blind Accessibility in Games

CHAPTER 9

Basic Principles of Blind Accessibility

ALRIGHT, IT'S TIME TO really, truly break down exactly how you can make your games accessible to the blind. You will have read some of this information already if you've read the first part of this book, as I occasionally used these bits of advice in order to help illustrate a point, but this is where you can find them all collected for your convenience. We're going to start with some basic principles, as the title of this chapter states, but then we'll break it down into specific genres and types of games. Hopefully, we cover the game you're thinking about or working on. Maybe reading about how you could do this inspires you to make a brand-new game. Hey, I can dream, can't I? I want to play more games! Anyway, enough introduction. Let's get to it.

The first and most basic principle of blind accessibility is that it's all about information. When you can't see, and you're trying to play a video game that doesn't contain blind accessibility-specific features, you are probably missing quite a bit of information that is conveyed visually to the player. That is the consideration you should start with when thinking about making your game accessible to the totally blind. Don't start with the how, because we're not there yet. We'll get to that. Start with this consideration of information. Ask yourself what information the blind are missing in your game or will miss in the game you want to make. Really think about this, as the smallest barrier could prevent us from playing your

DOI: 10.1201/9781003433750-11

game entirely. I gave up on the fighting game MultiVersus, not because of the gameplay, but because I couldn't get past the license agreement. That is not a joke. In VR games, the biggest blocker for blind play, in my opinion, is the non-universal way in which VR games are configured. Uncertainty about how to configure individual VR games on first launch almost always leads to unplayability right off the bat. This is Also not a joke. Consider everything you can. You will likely miss something along the way, but doing your best to take everything into consideration as early as possible makes it more likely that you can fix something you missed later.

As a side note, that's a good principle for general accessibility. Start thinking about it as early as possible. Building accessibility, any kind of accessibility, into your design from the ground up not only makes the overall process easier, but usually results in a better experience for everyone, not just the disabled. Remember that accessible design is good design. Here's the thing, though. This isn't an argument against patching in accessibility. I'm not trying to tell you not to patch accessibility into an existing game. I think you absolutely should if you have the resources to do so. However, I am saying that it will be more difficult, as you may have to rewrite some systems to accommodate new features. It can be done, though. There are examples I've already given in this book (Sequence Storm, Brok the InvestiGator), that have done an absolutely stellar job of this. So, if you have a game that's already out there, I would still say consider it if it makes sense for you to do so. But if you're about to start a new project, maybe focus on making that project as accessible as it can be.

Alright, back to total blind accessibility. The second basic principle of blind accessibility is narration, narration, narration. Almost every game these days has some sort of text element, even if it's just the main menu, and we should have access to all of them. Sure, there are exceptions here, as there are exceptions to every rule. Journey, for instance, would probably require little to no narration at all to be fully blind accessible, because the game itself doesn't possess much text. But for the most part, a good step one in the building process should be to ensure that any text element you have is going to be narrated to us in some form. This can be achieved in many ways, from human-voiced narration, (expensive but awesome depending on the game), to adding screen reader support for a user's existing screen reader (easiest on PC but possible for Xbox and PS5), to prerecording text to speech files as we did in TLOU2 (not ideal for every game since it doesn't account for anything that might come from outside the game world like player names in a multiplayer game), to adding in your own, hand-crafted text to speech solution, (potentially difficult, but worth looking into on a game for, say, the Nintendo Switch). One of these things, or even a combination of them, can lead you to full access to these elements. Diablo IV, for instance, has a robust narration system, including screen reader support, but certain journals and notes you pick up are still voiced by human voice actors, as they always have been throughout the series. This still counts as access. Think carefully about your solution for this, as it isn't likely to change once you've adopted something.

Sticking on this narration point for a moment, I'd also like to advise you not to over-narrate. There are some games with great narration overall, but over-narration slows things down. For example, one of my early criticisms of As Dusk Falls was a particular bit of narration in its options menu. Every time you moved over an option, narration would start off by saying "setting," followed by the option's name. This actually hurt more than it helped, as it made it nearly impossible to go through menus quickly to find what we were looking for. We always had to wait through "setting" before we could know for certain which option we were highlighting.

It's also worth considering the narration order. The order in which the narrated text is spoken does matter, so when narrating any given screen, make sure you consider what information is the most important, and narrate that first. This again allows the blind player to move quickly through screens, especially once they get a handle on them. Then, if you have less important information narrated after the important stuff, it feels a lot more like a choice the blind player makes to hear that information, should they want to, or not hear it and move on since they heard the most important information already. Of course, narration order applies to all aspects of narration, including that which happens during gameplay, but I'm not going to get too deep into that just yet since that can be very game-specific.

Next up in our basic principles list is input. Remember, especially if you're making a game on PC, that a blind person likely doesn't use a mouse. Many blind people don't even have one. They control their computers entirely with their keyboard. Therefore, to help guarantee blind accessibility, your game should have keyboard or controller support. These are interfaces that can be understood by a blind person much more easily than a mouse, and if done right, can give us the kind of interface to your game that we need. This brings me to my next point.

This isn't so much as a principle as it is a bit of unashamed begging. Please, please do not require cursor movement with a controller. By this, I mean that we should not, at any point, have to use the thumbsticks to move an actual cursor around in a nonlinear fashion, desperately hoping that we eventually land on the thing we're looking for. That's the whole reason we don't use mice. It's not fun. Instead, moving through items should snap to each one as it did in the old days of video games before anyone thought to put a cursor on consoles. If we go down, it should jump to the next item in that direction. Same for left or right. You get the idea. If you must have some cursor movement, such as a map you want a player to be able to move around freely, then I recommend using the D-pad on controller, or alternate keys on a keyboard to allow for snap movement on that screen, while a sighted player is still free to use the mouse or thumbsticks to get the freedom they desire. Although in the specific case of a map, especially a large one, I am going to recommend a different system entirely, but we'll get to that later.

The next principle is navigation. A blind player must be able to navigate your world, whatever that means for you. I'm not going to get too deeply into this one here, as it depends very, very much on the game, but it is something I will be focusing heavily on in future chapters. Just keep that in mind as a general rule. You're going to have to find a way for a blind person to get through your world, large or small, and you can do that, but how you do it is going to depend on what kind of game you're building.

Lastly, I offer you a principle that applies to accessibility in general. Remember that every game is different. If you're designing a game, even one that fits into a specific well-established genre, you probably still want to be innovative on some level with your creation. Whatever that innovation is, it will make your game stand out, but it will also mean a new accessibility consideration or two. So, this one is also a reminder that this book is intended to be a guideline, but not to be a replacement for working with accessibility consultants. I encourage you to get creative, and to be innovative, because that's how progress is made in this industry. However, let us help you. We want your game to be accessible to us, and we can help ensure that happens. Take all you can from this book, because that's what it's here for, but also involve the disabled in consulting on and testing for your game. I promise it's worth it.

That covers the basics. I hope by this point you have built a foundation of understanding regarding blind accessibility and the types of things we need in order to play your game. Now, though, it's time to start breaking it down. It's time to get specific. Not all of the upcoming chapters will be relevant to you, but still, they might be worth reading just to get an idea of the different approaches each game type requires. First, we'll take a deeper look into one of the principles we just talked about. Let's go!

CHAPTER 10

Every Game Is Different

IN CASE YOU'RE STARTING here, I'll go over this main point once again. Every game is different. When you make a game, even if it fits into a particular genre, you want it to be different in some way. You want it to stand out, and so you want to be innovative. This is why I continue to stress the need to still work with the disabled when designing accessibility features. This book is a guideline for blind accessibility, and I hope it's a good one, but it isn't intended as a substitute for working with us to help optimize your accessibility efforts. OK, now that's out of the way, let's dive into this idea a bit more.

Before we get to the subject of individual game innovation, we can talk a bit more about the general idea of every game being different. Each type of game requires different approaches to accessibility. You'll note that all the subsequent chapters really break down these ideas, but here are a few examples.

Visual novels are potentially some of the easiest games to make blind accessible. Most of the time, all you really need is narration support. After all, a visual novel is primarily text, so there's no need for any kind of navigational assist or aim assist or anything of that nature. However, I say most of the time because some visual novels do go an extra step or two. Some have mini-games that you must complete in order to progress the story, and depending on the nature of the mini-game, some accessibility may need to be considered. But that's where your innovation comes in, right?

Fighting games are a pretty good next step on the ladder, as they tend to need very little. Using Mortal Kombat 1 as an example, we've got audio

DOI: 10.1201/9781003433750-12

cues for different types of attacks, for distance to the opponent, for blocking, for being in the corner, and so on, we've got narration, of course, and we've got audio description. That is several features for sure, but it's not nearly as many as The Last of Us, for example. Fighting games have a certain level of natural accessibility due to their very closed nature. Most fighting games are 2D fighters, meaning you're only ever moving in two dimensions. You're always right across from your opponent, no matter where they happen to be, so the blind are never left wondering where they are. Sometimes there's a question of which side an opponent is on, but that is often solved with correct stereo panning. If your character audio is individualized, all attacks, grunts, movement sounds and so on being unique to each character, then we can just use stereo panning to determine which side our opponent is on and even how far away they are. Then, just having this good sound design means we can easily learn the sounds a character and their attacks make. We have considered this to be OK for quite a while, but of course, all the additional features I mentioned above take things to the next level. Imagine not being able to browse a character's move list, right there in the pause menu, in your favorite fighting game. That's the difference. The difference between learning moves via tons of online sources, some of which just take down moves incorrectly, and being able to use the same in-game list everyone else is using.

Now, let's talk about how an open world game is different from an action-adventure title like TLOU2. They share many of the same needs and features, but navigational needs vary a great deal between the two of them. The nav assist system we have in TLOU2 and TLOU1 works because those games are mostly linear, some levels being what we call Wide Linear, where you have some choice of where to go, but not much. But in an open-world game, additional considerations must be made. How do we navigate a world where a sighted player would have complete freedom? How do we deal with the monstrous scale and scope of the open world? Don't worry, the answers to these questions are coming. For now, the question illustrates the example. You couldn't just slap TLOU2 nav assist into an open-world game and call it good. It wouldn't be enough.

Approaches to specific elements can also require you to look harder at their accessibility. I spoke of the Invisible While Prone feature earlier in this book, so I won't go into great detail again here, but I will say that part of the reason that feature was decided upon was simply that you COULD go prone. The other aspects aside, it made sense. The act of going prone indicates stealth, so why not attach the method of going stealth as a blind player to that? It's something a player can follow. When TLOU1 came around, featuring a character that couldn't go prone, it just continued to make sense from a button perspective to leave it as it was. But all of this was very specific to this game. That's what I mean when I say every game is different.

Accessibility shouldn't just exist. It should fold into the game as seamlessly as possible. Obviously, that won't always be perfectly seamless, but things should make as much sense as they can. That helps to create immersion in your world. When you think about accessibility, think about your implementation choices and how they relate to your game overall. Maybe sometimes a different approach to the same feature makes sense for you, because it fits better in your game's world. It's a lot to think about, which is, again, why this book is merely a guideline. Now, though, let's start getting specific. Now it's time to talk about individual mechanics and how to make them blind accessible. I will drill down into each, and even provide a little example, but remember that it is just an example, and it does not mean you should implement things the same way in your game. Alright, enough of all that. Let's drill down!

CHAPTER 11

Narration

WE'VE TALKED A LOT about narration in this book so far. It is, after all, one of the basic principles of blind accessibility in games. Some of the information in this chapter has been dispersed throughout other sections, so some of it may be familiar, but there should be enough here to take something more from. Let's talk narration!

Narration is a great first step in making your game accessible. Some games may only need narration to become fully blind accessible, such as some visual novels. Either way, the rule of thumb here is pretty simple. Every text element should be narrated. If something is communicated to a sighted player with text, the blind should have access to it in some way. Sometimes this means having a specialized button for something (checking your stats, for example), and sometimes narration should just be automatic, such as when the player navigates into a new zone or level. There are exceptions to this, believe it or not, but those are defined in very specific situations. But as much as possible, narrate everything.

Narration can also mean multiple things. Some developers have chosen to rely entirely on human-voiced narration. This is most common in audio-only games. Games like Evidence #111, an interactive audio drama, don't actually support VoiceOver (the iPhone's screen reader), at all, because they don't need to. They built custom gestures for interaction, and all narration is handled by a human voice. When making a choice, the choices are laid out to you by the characters, with an early-game tutorial on how to make a choice when one comes up. This is still narration. In choice-based games like this, a sighted player might see two or three

DOI: 10.1201/9781003433750-13

choices pop up on screen and click on one to select it. Having a character tell us what our choices are is still giving us that information, and still counts.

Of course, narration using human voices gets more and more expensive the bigger the game is, and it also has certain disadvantages. For example, if your game has any kind of dynamic element, such as messages of the day, or constantly updating content, or if it uses a user-entered name, be it a gamer tag or a character name, human narration just may not work as a solution. It may not even be advisable if your character has a large number of modifiable stats, just because recording all the permutations of those things alone may be horrendously expensive. Of course, you could do a bit of both, as the Diablo series does. Diablo IV has synthesized narration for a ton of game elements, but as has been true for the entire Diablo series, the collectable lore books you can find throughout the game are narrated by human voice acting. This is fine, and I would say it even helps add to the immersion. It also helps separate the lore from the narration you're also hearing, which is important in that game because lore like that will continue playing even during combat.

So now we get to synthesized narration, or narration using text to speech. This is a less expensive, but more complex form of narration, as you must find a text-to-speech solution that fits your players and your game. There are multiple factors to consider here, such as how many platforms your game will be on, and which platforms, because text-to-speech development can get more difficult the more platforms you have to make it work on. If a game is platform-exclusive, you could just focus your efforts on that platform's available screen reader solutions. Xbox, for instance, has a built-in screen reading solution called Narrator. Since Xbox runs a version of Windows, building something with Narrator support may cover your PC bases as well. The PS5 also has a built-in screen reader, which, although I'm not completely clear on this, seems to now be accessible to developers via an API, as I have encountered a couple of games that use it (Diablo IV, and Gotham Knights). So, if a game is PS5 exclusive, that may be the easiest way to go. If your game is exclusive to PC, the best way to support narration may just be to support existing PC screen readers like NVDA and Jaws. There is a library called Tolk that will make doing this very easy in most cases, but we're also now seeing some in-engine support. Unreal, for instance, has screen reader support as something you can set up within the engine, and has already been demonstrated in Halo: The

Master Chief Collection. Unity is working on the same kind of support, but even now, there are multiple plugins that have been created for Unity to add screen reader functionality to them. One was created by Apple, allowing Unity developers to support VoiceOver on iPhones, but one was created by PopCap Games, and seems to be a more universal plugin for multiple platforms, as it has been used for games on mobile as well as PC and console. A good example of the use of this latter plugin is Alt Frequencies. There aren't any good examples of the Apple plugin as of this writing, as it has only been demonstrated and is not used in any game I am aware of.

Another option that exists is the use of a service called ReadSpeaker, which can be found at readspeaker.com. This service offers a couple of different solutions that would work for narration in games. First, you can have ReadSpeaker produce audio files for each string that requires narration. This is effectively The Last of Us method, and can work in a lot of cases, but again, you must consider how much dynamic content your game contains. Will your game use character or player names, or have content that changes throughout its life cycle? Then narration done this way may not be advisable for you. You could always get new audio files for the new strings for updating content, but those user-generated bits of text will get you every time. Still, if your game does not contain these things, this is a perfectly acceptable form of narration and has the advantage of working on all platforms.

ReadSpeaker's second option is a plugin that can hook right into your game and produce text to speech in real time. As I understand it, should you choose to work with them, they will help ensure their plugin can work with your game and help with implementation if necessary. The idea here would be that their plugin would fold directly into your game's code, meaning that once again it could theoretically work on all platforms, and with none of the disadvantages of narration via audio files. Let me also just say that this isn't an intentional advertisement for ReadSpeaker, they are just one of the only companies offering a service like this in the gaming space. Definitely worth looking into, though.

Lastly, there is the difficult, but doable method of building your own narration solution into your game. There are some text to speech synthesizers that can be licensed for fairly cheap, and you could choose to hook them up to code you simply write yourself. This is probably the most difficult approach, but again, like some other solutions, it would theoretically work on all platforms your game is to be released on. Some studios like Ubisoft have taken this approach, and many of their games now have fairly good narration, such as Assassin's Creed: Valhalla and Watchdogs: Legion.

All the methods of narration I've listed above are valid, depending on the type of game being built. Choose whichever works for you, but no matter which you choose, follow that golden rule of blind accessibility—narrate everything.

Now that we've established pretty solidly that everything should be narrated, let's talk about other narration considerations. The first is customizability. If your narration method is simply supporting other screen readers, you don't have to worry much about this. The player can simply configure their screen reader with the settings they like, and those settings should carry over to your game. But if you're using text to speech of some other kind, you may want to consider allowing people to adjust the rate of speed, the volume, or even the pitch. When multiple voice options are available, you may want to allow players to configure that, too. This isn't always possible (if you're using prerecorded audio files, for example), but when it is, it should at least be a consideration. Allowing a user to customize their experience to best fit them is a key component of accessible game development, and you'll quickly learn that most blind people set narration speeds much faster than their typical defaults.

The ultimate convergence of these things is probably the Microsoft Narrator API, which allows you to not only check a user's existing narrator settings, but also to establish different settings on a per-game basis. For this reason, we were able to make Forza Motorsport's narration suite extremely comprehensive. Players have access to narrator settings like speed and volume within the game itself and can even select from every available Microsoft Speech API voice in their region. Doing this within the game will only modify the settings of the game and won't affect their Narrator system settings on Xbox or PC. It's pretty neat to allow users to create that kind of separation, though of course, that can't apply to every game.

OK, so everything should be narrated, and narration should be customizable where possible. Great. Now you must tackle the shockingly difficult question of HOW everything should be narrated. Keep in mind that the blind player does not get a constant view of the screen like a sighted player does. So, what do you narrate on each screen, and when? These are very important questions, and it is possible to do this in a way that is not necessarily wrong, but a worse experience for the player. And no, the answer is not that you just reread the entire screen every time the player makes a move. We're going to get into this now so you can ensure your screens are narrated in the most user-friendly, blind-friendly way possible.

First, you need to figure out what is the most important thing is to narrate in the current moment. A basic example of this is when the player's focus enters a new screen. Let's take a game's main menu. The game loads, and the main menu appears. What does narration say? Maybe it says the game's title, "Super Epic RPG 3: Doughnuts to Dollars"), and maybe not. This is a developer preference. The way I see it, if your game opens with a splash screen showing the title as you transition into the main menu, then yeah, you should narrate it. Once that's done, you might say something like "Main menu," to indicate which screen the player has arrived on. Every screen the player might need narration to navigate through should have a title like this, but it only needs to be announced upon entering that screen. Then what do you do? Do you narrate the entire menu? No. Focus on the moment. Narrate the option the player is on currently to establish for them exactly where their focus is. Let them move through and explore the menu themselves and learn it, allowing them to navigate it much faster in future sessions.

Now let's switch from the main menu to a more complex menu, the options menu. Some of these things can apply to a main menu as well, but I think the concept of an options menu will demonstrate this point best. We're still talking about narration order here, but in a menu like options or settings, things get a lot more complex. Before you read on, stop and consider how you currently think a menu like this should be narrated. Have you considered? Good. Let's see how right you were. I'll leave it to you to keep a score card.

When the player enters this menu, first, you want to tell them where they are. "Options," or "Options Menu," or "Settings." You get the idea. The next item depends on how you've split the options menu screen. In menus with fewer options, there may be no need to categorize them, but if there is, make sure the player knows next which category they are currently in. Then, you read the option they are currently highlighting. Follow that up with its value, because that is the next item of direct importance to a player who might later do this quickly. After the value, then you read the option's tool tip, if it has one. Here's an example of how this should sound.

"Settings menu. Appearance. Doughnut detail: High. Adjusting this setting adjusts the visual detail applied to all in-game doughnuts. At a low setting, only their shape will be visible. When set to ultra, it will be possible to detect every individual sprinkle."

Ordering things this way allows the player to skip the tooltip if they don't need to hear it (if they're already familiar with what the option does and just want to change it, for example), and move onto the next option. Of course, this is a hint that, if the player presses anything, narration should be appropriately interrupted, and the new relevant information should be narrated. If they pressed the down arrow, they'd probably hear the next option in the menu. If they pressed right, though, they would only need to hear what this option was changed to, which in this case is "ultra." Don't think you have to reread the entire option if its value is changed. Let the interruption of narration be the player's doing. It's their choice, and they will have their reasons for cutting narration off. Also, as they move down through options in the same category, don't feel the need to read that category over and over. Categories only need to be read when they change. So, if a player moves down to the next option (which is Chocoholic Filter in my imaginary game in case you're curious), there isn't a need for narration to say "appearance' again, because we're still in that category. Just narrate that option, its value, and its tooltip.

Another key thing here is not to over-narrate. This is harder to avoid than it might seem if you use the Microsoft Narrator API, which has a smart default system that tries to figure out how to narrate things for you. In my opinion, this system's defaults over narrate significantly. For instance, the same settings menu example we gave earlier would sound a bit more like this if you were using that API on its default levels.

"Settings menu. Group: Appearance. Option: Doughnut Detail: option 1 of 6. Value selector. Current value: high. Adjusting this setting adjusts the visual detail applied to all in-game doughnuts. At a low setting, only their shape will be visible. When set to ultra, it will be possible to detect every individual sprinkle."

Whoa, right? That is a lot. In my opinion, it's far too much. The exception here could be the number of options in the menu, which some players may want. Me, I never minded not having that piece of information. I want menu narration to be quick and concise. As I work more and more with each menu, I'll figure it out. But that's just me, and one of the greatest things I've learned in this career is that you cannot design for the super user.

I'm going to use As Dusk Falls to demonstrate a point about over narration. As Dusk Falls has some of the best in-game narration ever, (more on that in a bit), but its menus, specifically its settings menu, leave something to be desired. It's not narrated badly, but it does have one particularly glaring problem. As you browse through it, the first thing you hear upon highlighting each setting is the word "setting." Why is this problematic? Because ultimately, you want your players to become familiar with your menus, so they might browse them quickly. The first time they go through a menu with narration, they will likely listen to all the information provided for them. You don't want them to have to do that every time, however. Narrating "setting" before each item makes it highly likely that a blind user will stay on options longer than they need to because they must wait until that word finishes to get confirmation of which option they're highlighting. It becomes impossible to skim the menu this way to find the thing you're looking for. That is over narration.

One thing to keep in mind going forward is that the concepts of narration ordering we went over a bit ago apply to every narrated screen in your game. This will be a lot of work with a big, complex game, but I can assure you it is important work. To put this in perspective, I was asked during development to approve the way each and every screen in Forza Motorsport was narrated, because we had systems in place to change it all around if necessary. This even applied to narration that took place during gameplay, which is a wonderful segway into my next topic—prioritization.

Narration during gameplay can be challenging but is still very necessary when following the golden rule that is "narrate everything." How you pick your narration priority, though, will depend on the game and the specific experience you want players to have during gameplay. In Forza Motorsport, we have a queueing system in place. Our narration is sent through the game's VO system, allowing us to treat it like other VO, and letting us decide when it should and shouldn't play. For instance, when in the early stages of the game, those times when tutorial messages, which are VO lines delivered by your race coach, are still playing, those lines are prioritized over narration, because they need to play at specific times or risk becoming irrelevant. So, they play first, and any narration that would play at the same time queues up behind them. However, as you get further on, passing beyond tutorial time, narration gets prioritized over some VO because it might contain information the blind player might want more in the moment, such as their lap time upon completing a lap, or acknowledgment of the XP they just gained for taking a corner well.

In The Last of Us Part II, and then subsequently part 1, we took a different approach. We prioritize via audio ducking. If the player is not in combat, and screen narration and character VO are set to be played at the same time, the narration is ducked in favor of the character voices because The Last of Us is extremely narrative-driven, and we don't want the player to miss that character dialog. However, if the blind player is in a combat encounter when narration and VO would play at the same time, we do the opposite, ducking all voices in favor of narration, because now the important details are the player's health, ammo count, and so on.

As you can see, prioritization can be important, but as with most things, it depends very much on the game. Remember when I said that As Dusk Falls has some of the best in-game narration ever? Part of the reason for that is that they don't really have to worry about prioritization, since their game is essentially an interactive movie with occasional choices and quicktime events. Still, that doesn't diminish the impact their narration has on the game. If something needs to be narrated, it just is. Title cards as you move into new scenes, button presses for those quicktime events, and even text messages sent and received by each character. All of these things are narrated exactly when they should be, which is of course immediately when they happen. It's fantastic and really helps immerse us in the game.

One more thing for you, visual novel creators out there. While all the ways listed above for adding narration to your game can apply to you, I want you to know that, if you use the Ren'Py engine for the creation of your visual novel, you will have access to an in-engine self-voicing mode. Many games support this already, such as Arcade Spirits and Blake: A Visual Novel, so I recommend looking to them for inspiration. Of course, that doesn't mean you have to use that engine for your game, it's just a way you can make blind accessibility a bit easier. You can even label any clickable segment of the screen, so those moments where the blind have to look around at objects in a room are even easier.

That's narration. Follow the golden rule, figure out your narration solution, your ordering, your prioritization, and you are well on your way to making your game blind accessible. Still, we've got a long way to go. Let's keep going, shall we?

CHAPTER 12

Navigation and Traversal

Lots of games today are built in worlds players can explore, sometimes to their heart's content. Some worlds are enormous constructs of epic proportions, known as open worlds. They are going to have their very own chapter later. For now, we're going to cover the basics of helping a blind person navigate your world, as, once again, there are multiple ways to approach this. No matter what, though, unless your game contains no navigation at all, such as an interactive experience like As Dusk Falls or Stray Gods, the blind player is going to need help with this. Let's discuss how you can make this happen.

The style of navigation you use depends on the types of navigation required and, in some cases, the complexity of your game. The larger and more complex your game world, the more complex it will be to provide true navigation assistance. Of course, even a small but complex world presents its own challenges, such as a platformer. We're going to talk about all these things, don't worry.

I'm going to start with a fairly complex example because it's one that exists right now, and thus it's something you can reference for yourself. I'm going to start with, you guessed it, The Last of Us Parts 1 and 2. How do we navigate through this game's world? Allow me to explain.

The navigation assist system of The Last of Us was an enormous and complex effort. The short version is that when you press L3, an audio cue plays in the direction of your objective, and the camera turns to face it. So, pressing L3 while pushing forward will get you where you're going, the audio cue helping to signify when you've taken a turn just

DOI: 10.1201/9781003433750-14

so you, the player, know when that happens. However, under the hood, it is much, much more complex than that. Every single time the player presses L3, a ray is cast from the player to the next hand-crafted point, whether that's a wall, or a doorway, or even just a reasonable distance from the player. Yes, you read that right. The maps for The Last of Us Part II, and then the Part I remake, were marked up for navigational assistance by hand. This is because there's an inherent problem with only using the camera method. That problem is that your objective may be, and in fact almost always is, on the other side of at least one wall or barrier of some kind. Using a method that only turns the camera and points toward your objective is almost assuredly going to inevitably guide your player into a bunch of walls sooner or later, even though it might appear to work for a little bit.

Let me give you a painful example of this. Marvel's Spiderman: Miles Morales on PS5 has a navigational assistance feature. Pretty cool, right? In fact, I was able to complete the entire introduction to the game on my own without sighted assistance. After the intro was over, though, I quickly learned why I was able to complete it, and it was the same reason I was able to complete SOME of the intro of Spiderman 2018 Remastered, which also has the same nav assist feature. The reason is… You're Spiderman. Because you're Spiderman, an as-the-crow-flies navigation style works… when you're out in the open. Swinging through the city is fine because nothing is going to stop you. You're Spiderman. But once you move into buildings, or once you have to do any kind of ground navigation at all, really, you quickly fall victim to the fact that this nav assist wasn't scripted out and marked up by hand. It is only using the camera method, meaning you're going to hit a lot of walls if you're not swinging. This is what I mean by painful. To start things off by succeeding, especially in Miles Morales where I completed the entire intro, then to literally hit a wall, multiple times, just when I was starting to have hope that maybe, maybe I could work my way through this game. It hurt.

Puzzles are a thing we'll talk about in more detail later, but I should note that the nav assist in The Last of Us also covers puzzles via the use of careful scripting. In order to get blind players through, you are guided to each point of interaction in order to complete a puzzle. Again, we'll go into this later as it's not the only possibility for puzzles, but for now, it's worth noting that that is an option for nav assist if you feel it makes sense for your game.

The next bit of The Last of Us' navigational assistance is actually a separate feature called traversal assistance. On the surface, this feature will automatically vault over certain objects to assist you with getting to your objectives faster. However, it does more than that. For instance, if your character isn't quite lined up with a jump point when you get the prompt, traversal assistance will take control for just a second, turn your character to properly face the jump, then execute it. This helps with things like jumping through windows. It also helps with the completion of sprint jumps, and certain puzzles where specific movement is required. It's a feature that couple with navigational assistance well because we still cannot see the world around us, and don't know how you want us to get to these places. Helping us in this way, or with audio cues (which we'll also get to later), is definitely advised for games with all sorts of navigational challenges.

The last part of navigational assistance in The Last of Us is our enhanced listen mode. This allows you to scan the area for items or enemies, and then press a button combination, R1 plus L3, to pathfind to those instead of your primary objective. This allows the blind player to explore their environment, with certain limitations, in order to find the loot they need to survive, as well as the game's many collectable items. The pathfinding still uses the mapping system marked up by hand but plots a course through the appropriate points to get you to the item or enemy you scanned. I mentioned limitations, though, because the system is limited by two major things. First, the maximum 30-meter scan radius. Some of the maps, especially in The Last of Us Part II, are absolutely gigantic, and there is a significant distance between potentially interactable or collectable items. It is quite easy, therefore, to miss many things through your journey. Secondly, it's limited by the fact that the pathfinding always guides you to the closest thing in the scan. If that happens to be a story interactable that advances the story in such a way as to prevent you from collecting the other things in the area, then so be it. Also, if you're surrounded by items, one of which happens to be a collectable you really want, you cannot prioritize the collectable. It is then possible that, once you've collected closest item after closest item again and again and again, you may now be more than 30 meters away from the collectable you really wanted in the first place. I still think the system is great for being one of the first of its kind, don't get me wrong, but I would highly suggest finding ways around such limitations for your players if you design a system like this.

One potential example you could look to for an improved navigational assist system is a game called 1428: Shadows Over Silesia. On the surface, their navigational assist works similarly to The Last of Us. You press a key, a sound plays, and you are turned to face your objective. The difference here is that you can change what that objective is in several ways. You can press keys to cycle between your active quests and side quests, and still other keys to cycle through interactable targets, including collectable loot and items, as well as conversations and story progression. When cycling, each target is announced, so we know what we'll be pathing toward if we begin pressing that key. The freedom of choice here is huge, as it allows us to decide at all times what we are heading toward, even if we still need a little help getting there.

1428: Shadows Over Silesia also uses another kind of navigational assist, specifically to allow us to just explore our environment without automatically turning toward everything. It uses specific audio cues to indicate walls near you. When active, a clicking sound plays in the direction of each wall in your immediate area. The further away the wall is, the slower and lower-pitched that clicking is. Because of this, we can walk along corridors and find turns and sometimes even hidden passages. Basically, if there is no clicking on one side, you're completely unblocked. If there is clicking, but it's low and slow, it might be a little side corridor that has a more hidden turn at its end, which you will only find if you head that way. Clicks like this can definitely be used in some games, but I wouldn't recommend it as the only navigational method if you do use them. It's a method that works very, very well inside buildings but doesn't work at all as soon as the player is in a wide-open environment. You could have a system like this monitor certain other things that aren't walls, of course. For example, a game that takes place in an urban environment could choose to identify roads or paths this way, monitoring the edges of the path rather than individual walls, but this is up to you, and what kinds of navigational assistance you think would work for your game. Creativity is encouraged, as long as you can help us get there.

Let's go through a couple of scenarios that do not exist as of this writing. These are ideas I've had for existing games and are good examples of how you could be creative with your nav assist. First, we're going back to Spiderman, the web-swinging sensation himself. Here's what I envision, going from basic to the coolest idea ever.

On the ground, you have a navigation system that is essentially an upgraded version of The Last of Us' nav assist. Something that allows you to scan an area and choose what you're navigating toward, or to head toward your objective if that is your desire. Once you've chosen your goal, you are helped to get there by both nav assist and traversal assist, as well as helpful audio cues that tell you if you need to hop over this thing, or climb this wall, and so on. Even if you need to do a little swinging to get to your objective, there is audio cue and traversal assistance for that. When you reach your objective, you are notified via audio, or maybe a little narration, depending on what your objective is. If it's an interactable object, we'd be given a prompt to interact with it. Pretty basic stuff based on what we've discussed so far, am I right? Now for the coolest idea ever. This is an idea I actually presented to Insomniac in the form of a very long-winded feedback email after trying to play Miles Morales, but as of this writing, it doesn't exist. Here goes.

Currently, in both Spiderman games that contain a nav assist feature, you activate it by pressing a key which turns the camera toward your objective, even while swinging. This often means a tight grip on your controller as you're trying to swing, do point to point web zips, and so on while also pressing this button over and over. But… What if it didn't have to be like that? What if you could swing, care-free and easy, and really feel like Spiderman, instead of having to be stressed out by a need to press your nav button over and over, and hoping you don't over shoot your target, and hoping desperately that it's actually working in the first place because how would you really know until you get there? Well, boy, do I have the solution for you. What if you somehow chose the point you intended to swing to (more on ideas for that in the open world section), and the game did some quick calculations for how you could get there, then generated a kind of drone. The drone could be invisible to save on graphical memory, but it would just need to exist as an object in the world, and more importantly, a sound source. This sound source would then become something you literally chase using positional audio. Now, I don't mean chase as in you'll lose it if you stop moving, I mean that it will always stay carefully ahead of you as you make your way toward your objective, remaining close enough to stay audible but far enough that you're always following it. You then swing through the city, chasing it down using positional audio and never having to press a button to reorient. When you were close enough to your objective, it would hover over it, and stay there, so you know exactly where you had to drop, and you'd know if you went past it. If this did somehow happen, you could still press a button to reorient toward it if needed (mostly just if you swung too fast and ended up too far away), but the fact that you would mostly not be relying on a button in this scenario would be so, so freeing. Then, once you landed on your objective point, (or once a cut scene triggered because you swung into the right spot), the objective drone would just be deleted, to be summoned during your next navigational need, which may be automatic as soon as the cut scene is over if your objective started a story sequence. You just wouldn't want the drone sound to be playing during a cut scene, so anyone who tries this, please delete it and recreate it when necessary. So, there it is, the coolest idea ever. Personally, I love it, but of course I would.

Navigational assistance methods like the ones described above may not always work. For instance, in a top-down game like Diablo IV, you don't really turn your character or the camera in the same way as happens in games like The Last of Us. So, how would a navigational assist work in a game like that? Well, you could always try the wall audio cue method, but of course, that ceases to work in open areas. My recommendation is to treat this like a ground version of my Spiderman idea, though the chase doesn't have to be exactly like a chase. Just play a sound in the direction the character has to go next in order to path their way to their current objective (this should be a constant, but nonintrusive sound so it can be followed but doesn't annoy the player) and have that sound change direction immediately when the player also should. Make sure the waypoint system underpinning all this is smart. Remember, you cannot hope to guide the player as the crow flies. The system must know where they have to go in order to eventually get where they need to go. If that involves finding a place to climb up first, your system should take them there first. This may require custom scripting in more complex areas, but that applies to any of these navigation methods.

Let's talk about a couple more scenarios. These are the kinds of things where a traversal assistance feature becomes handy. In many games, it is very possible for the player to fall to their death if they should, say, jump off the rooftop they find themselves on. We have to provide enough information and ways to avoid this if possible. There are a couple of options here as well. First, of course, I'll reference The Last of Us and talk about our ledge guard system. This system did two things. As the player approached a ledge, they could fall off safely if they so choose, they would hear an audio cue indicating a safe fall but would be prevented from falling for just a couple seconds unless they continued to hold forward, which the system would take as acknowledgment that they wanted to fall off that ledge. After all, there might be something down there. However, if the player approached a fall that would lead to death, another, more ominous and lower-pitched audio cue would play, and the player would be prevented from falling entirely unless they voluntarily pressed the jump button... for some reason. This was an effort to protect players from accidentally falling, not just to their death, but also if they weren't ready yet. Since the player in this case cannot see the ledges, they need to know if the path they're currently walking on is taking them toward one and be given the opportunity to change that if it's not something they wish to pursue. This system does that quite nicely.

There is another option, however, which I might recommend for a game that is intended to be more difficult. Audio games that have things like ledges and pits will use audio to indicate where those edges are, but not in the same way. Examples of this are Super Liam, Bokurano Debouken 2 and 3, and Monkey Business. As the player takes each step, additional audio will be applied if they are within a certain number of steps of an edge of some kind. The audio can differ depending on terrain, or severity of the fall, possibly even both. The point of this method, though, is that you're warning the player of an approaching edge, but you're not slowing them down in any way. What happens next is up to them, and their reaction time. This is perfectly viable, but again it may be a decision you make based on the experience you want players to have when playing your game.

Other types of traversals, climbing things, vaulting over things, ziplining from this rooftop to that one and so on, can be handled in a number of ways. You could simply provide appropriate audio cues to identify those spots, (more on those in the audio cues chapter), you could do it automatically based on the path the player is taking (though if you do this I suggest giving the player an option not to), or you could do a mix of both, such as we did with The Last of Us. TLOU will automatically vault you over small things, and jump up onto small things, but any jump that requires a major commitment, you will be prompted to complete with an audio cue. To be clear, though, you are prompted for every jump, but traversal assistance will take care of the little ones, usually before you can even press anything.

And that, folks, is navigational assistance. Just like with other accessibility features, consider your game, consider what the player needs, and create the best solution that fits both of those things best. Of course, audio cues can be their own kind of navigational assistance, among other things, which is why this is a perfect segway into our next chapter!

CHAPTER 13

Audio Cues

THE BEST WAY TO communicate something to a blind player in a game isn't always with narration. Narration is great, and much can be communicated that way, but sometimes you need something more. That's where audio cues come in. There are lots of reasons you would use an audio cue instead of, or to compliment, narration. First, positionality. The nice thing about audio cues is that, since they can be sound sources in your game world, the player will hear the audio cue positionally where they were meant to hear it. If an audio cue is telling a player to jump onto a ledge that is to their right while also being slightly in front of them, that's something you can communicate by attaching the cue to the ledge, and of course by using positional audio in your game to begin with. Side note, while you should include mono audio as a feature for the deaf/hard of hearing community, please avoid making your game entirely mono as a general rule. The audio is the closest thing the blind have to graphics, and positionality matters.

Second, audio cues can be used in places where narration might be speaking at the same time, thus communicating information more quickly. Let's say your player is walking along in your game world and decides to check their health status while continuing to walk toward their goal. As they listen to the readout, they will still get any navigational cues they need, since they're audio cues. Let's say that, while doing this, they approach an interactable object. Narration is still going on about their health, buff, and debuff status (perhaps they currently have the Stale debuff applied, which requires a ton of extra explanation). If the presence of this interactable object was communicated by

DOI: 10.1201/9781003433750-15

narration, it would either have to queue up behind the currently active narration, meaning the player would have to wait in order to hear it, or it would have to interrupt narration, which is almost never advisable unless the player makes a choice they know will interrupt it, such as choosing to go to the next item in a menu. See the previous chapter on narration for more on this. Either way, this doesn't make sense for the player. That is why you communicate that they've reached this object with an audio cue.

A third reason to use audio cues is in situations where information must be communicated more quickly than it could be with narration. This is especially true when you allow a player to adjust the speed of in-game narration (which you should), as players using slower speeds will have to wait longer for any information communicated that way. We're going to talk more about racing games in a later chapter, but there's a great example from Forza I want to use for this. In Forza, we give the players an audio cue to tell them at any given point how close they are to either edge of the track. You must react quickly in racing games, so just imagine if this were communicated by narration. "You're nearing the left edge of the track. Getting closer now. Boy oh boy, you are RIGHT on it!"

I'm exaggerating, but no matter what narration said, it would be too slow to communicate information like this, given how rapidly it can change. So instead, we use an audio cue that increases in speed and pitch the closer you get to the edge, becomes solid when you're right on the edge, and plays an additional sound if you go over. This is, believe me, very effective.

So, we've talked about the reasons to use audio cues. Now let's talk about what kinds of audio cues you might want to use. I've touched on some of these before in previous chapters, such as the navigational assistance chapter, but we'll go over them again here and provide more examples. In fact, let's start with navigation!

There are lots of ways audio cues can be used for navigational purposes. With The Last of Us, we used an audio cue when the player pressed the nav assist button so they could at least have an idea of which direction their objective was in compared to them. The audio cue was positional and would play in the direction the ray was cast, so it would also react as the camera turned in that direction. The idea was to give the player some indication of the world around them by auditorily describing the turns they were making. This is certainly not required to make a nav assist system work, as the system will be guiding the player anyway, but it's a nice gesture. Of course, anything the blind player activates should have some sort of audio cue so they can be sure it's working as intended.

Audio cues are also used in The Last of Us for traversal. Whenever the player must jump, crouch, use a melee attack to break a window, or climb a ladder, and so on and so on, this is indicated by an audio cue. This enables the player to maintain full interactivity while moving through a world they cannot see. Even when the player is using something like a navigational assistance feature, we still want them to have as much agency as we can give them. Giving them this information and letting them interact rather than simply doing everything for them is the better solution, and you can do that with appropriate audio cues.

Another game I've mentioned earlier, a game called 1428: Shadows Over Silesia, uses audio cues for identifying walls or barriers. This enables the blind to explore more freely rather than relying entirely on a nav assist to get around. In corridors, they can identify the walls on either side and know when there's an available turn based on when one of the wall cues fades or disappears. Even when outside, while exploring a town, for instance, they could identify the outer walls of buildings. You'll have to decide whether this kind of navigational audio can work for your game, though, as it wouldn't work in very open areas. Of course, you could combine this and a full nav assist to allow for exploration in some areas while also allowing for exploration in areas where it would work.

Audio cues could also be used as sound sources for a different kind of navigation. Oftentimes in audio games, every interactable thing in the game world is just a sound source, and we just track things by positionality. A door might be represented by a constant sound that just means door, and we just track it once we can hear it. This also applies to objects on the ground we can pick up. That being said, most audio games are not true 3D experiences, so again, using only this method may not always work, but it could be combined with other things as well.

I would like to approach the idea of using this kind of thing for something like a platformer. As fast-paced as some platformers are, something like this might be required to make one fully blind accessible. This hasn't yet been attempted with a video game platformer, hence my speculation, but it is the approach I would recommend starting with. Make the closest platforms, objects, and enemies sound sources with varying pitches to indicate height, allow the player to do some sort of scan around them so they can look further into the area, and you're on your way to making an accessible platformer. There would likely be a few more requirements, but that'd be a great start.

Let's talk a bit more about using audio cues for identification. I mentioned that audio cues were often attached to many things, turning them into sound sources, but how do you do that in a way to make sense? Well, for example, I will return once more to The Last of Us Parts I and II. In those games, we used something called sweeteners to identify specific things. In The Last of Us, you use the triangle button to interact with objects and pick up items, so the sound that indicated a triangle prompt was the baseline. Then, we would attach other sounds to that sound to get more specific. If you were being prompted to interact with a door, the triangle sound (a high-pitched ding) would play first, followed immediately by a separate short sound reminiscent of a door being pulled on. If you were interacting with a generator, the triangle prompt would play, followed immediately by a short version of a generator starter sound.

This also applies to collecting items. We had additional sweeteners for every item type you could collect, so you would know what you'd be picking up before you did so (unless of course you had auto-pickup on, in which case you'd be grabbing it all up anyway). Still, the sweeteners were there and would still be valuable if you had the maximum amount of an item you could hold, so you knew what you would need to use in order to collect the item you were standing in front of. The sweeteners we used for collecting items not only included different ammo types (arrows, bullets, fuel, and so on), but also every crafting material in the game, and even those rare cases where you were given a craftable item for free. It's all there. If a blind player must press the triangle, they will almost always know exactly why.

We can tie this back to navigation as well, as sweeteners were also used there. The button to climb a ladder was the same as the jump button (X), and so we applied a sweetener to the X or jump prompt that sounds a bit like a ladder being shaken a little bit to indicate there was a ladder to climb. Same with ropes, a mechanic that only appears in The Last of Us Part II, as well as gaps you need to squeeze through, which also require the same button press. Still more sweeteners are applied to puzzle-related notifications, such as when to place a ladder or plank. In short, sweeteners are powerful tools you can use to vastly increase the usage you can get out of your audio cues.

Next, I want to bring up the idea of audio cues for status. Sure, it's nice to be able to check one's health with narration to get an exact representation of where your health is, 73%, for instance, but sometimes you just want to know that your health is getting a bit low. This can be achieved via an audio cue, such as a heartbeat that increases in speed, which is a popular choice even for games that aren't blind accessible. But your character's health isn't the only status you might consider.

Games like Destiny 2 and Deadpool, both of which are also not blind accessible, use audio cues to help with your current ammunition count. Deadpool adds a couple of little beeps that play when you're firing the last few bullets in a clip, and Destiny 2 increases the clicks of your trigger when you are low on ammo. Both things are very useful ways of providing this information even to sighted people, as it prevents them from having to constantly watch their ammo count, but something like this could just as easily serve the blind as well. Audio cues like these are just more proof that accessible design is good design.

This idea goes even further, though. The Diablo series has, for the last couple of games, had subtle audio for many of its buffs. Be a sorcerer in Diablo III and cast frost armor, and you may notice a constant sound playing around your character while it's active. Diablo IV does this all over the place, including buffs created by shrines you find as you wander the world. It's just another way to communicate the information on a screen that shows when a buff is active. You could also do the same to indicate when a buff or debuff expires as well. And to expand upon this a bit further, why not throw an audio cue on cooldowns for things that have them? If your game has a lot of cooldowns, you could make a sound for each one so the player would always know when it wore off. Of course, each cooldown sound should be auditorily related to its buff sound so they would be easily identifiable and learnable.

Remember when I mentioned Destiny 2 and Deadpool above, talking about how they had useful audio cues even though they themselves are not blind accessible? I want to be clear that that happens a lot. We will use whatever audio you create. Accessible design is good design, and the more you try to fold your game's existing audio into that philosophy, creating natural audio cues, the better. If you read the first half of this book, you know that this is basically how we used to play all video games. Analyzing the sound, picking out what we could use to help us… The individual character voices the first Killer Instinct had, and now basically all fighting games have, is technically a helpful audio cue. It cues us into which character is which and, in the moment, just who is taking that massive punch to the face. Audio is important, folks. It's just as important as graphics.

Let me give you another example. Kingdom Hearts is one of my favorite games that isn't accessible. Well, combat is accessible thanks to its lock-on system, but that's another story. The thing I want to talk about is a subtle audio cue Square Enix decided to use in this game that wasn't something they had to do, but the fact that they did is pretty awesome. In Kingdom Hearts, your main character Sora wields a weapon called a Keyblade. As you progress through the game, you get several different versions of the Keyblade, often related to certain characters or worlds. The cool thing here, though, is that each individual Keyblade you get has a completely different sound set attached to it. Every swing with each one sounds different. Every successful strike sounds different. And craziest of all, the key blade has a sort of jouncing along sound that plays while you walk, you know, as if your weapon was juttering a little each time you took a step. Well, that sound is ALSO different for every single Keyblade. It's an incredible bit of attention to auditory detail that I absolutely love. We did this in The Last of Us as well, as the sounds your character makes while walking or crawling can be slightly different depending on the weapon you're holding at the time.

One more note about what your audio cues should sound like. Honestly, it's up to you, just as long as you're willing to teach blind players what your audio cues mean. This could be done with an audio glossary containing each audio cue along with a description of its meaning, as in The Last of Us, but it can also be placed in the appropriate tutorial messages in-game, and/or played when the player adjusts options related to each sound as in Forza Motorsport. The point is, as long as you teach players somehow, it's up to you what audio cues sound like. They don't necessarily have to be sounds that sound connected to your game world, though if you can pull that off, great. But sometimes, it is helpful to have a sound that kind of falls outside your usual soundscape just to make it stand out more. Again, it is up to you.

With The Last of Us, we went with a melodic approach. Most audio cues are in the same key and are different types of reverberating dinging sounds, which separates them a bit from the game world but gives them their own kind of theme that players can follow. This turned out to be both a good thing and a bad thing because I did witness multiple players confusing the higher-pitched version of the jump cue, the version that plays when your jump target is above you, for some other cue they hadn't heard yet. Their confusion made sense because all the cues were in the same key, and our higher versions just shot the cue an octave up. I provide this example just as an additional thing to consider, but I stress one more time that this is up to you. Provide us with the information that makes sense to provide with audio, and we won't care much about what sounds you use as long as you teach them to us.

Basically, it all comes down to this. Just like haptics, just like narration, audio cues are another channel through which you could provide information to your blind players. We've discussed the different types, the reasons why you would do this, and provided examples of ways in which implementation could be achieved. Now it's up to you. Fill your game with audio, teach your blind players, and set them loose. Whatever you do with audio, I promise you they'll be the ones who notice the most.

CHAPTER 14

The Power of Good Audio Design

We spent a long time talking about audio cues, and some of this chapter is going to expand on some of the things we talked about there, but this time, we're focusing on the power of generally good audio design that goes beyond cues created specifically for accessibility. These are the things some audio designers are already doing, and if you're not, these things are worth your consideration, not just for accessibility but to improve the overall quality of your game's audio. I said it in the last chapter, and I will say it again to start this one. Audio is just as important as graphics. Audio designers, I'm on your side. Let's talk about how you can maximize the effectiveness of your audio while also promoting accessibility.

I think if we break down this idea, we can conclude that it's mostly about the little things. Really, truly great audio design seeks to add as much detail to a game's audio as the artists and animators do for its graphics. Taking an example, I brought up in the previous chapter, where Sora's Keyblade audio in Kingdom Hearts changes depending on which Keyblade is equipped, right down to the walking sound as it jutters with him, you can see what I mean. The inclusion of these extra-specific details served as an alternate channel of information for the blind. Suddenly, I could tell what key blade someone playing Kingdom Hearts was using at any given time.

DOI: 10.1201/9781003433750-16

Let's go for another, more recent example. Hades, the rogue lite action game, has really good audio design in several ways. So good, in fact, that after a few minutes of listening to Hades being played by someone else for the first time, I knew I would be able to figure out how to play it, and I did, even before the accessibility mods were created. Let's get into the specifics of why that is.

The very first thing I noticed when I started listening to Hades was the sound that played when any creature spawned into the room you currently occupied. The hiss followed by a pop is not only distinctive but also positional, meaning that I knew exactly where enemies were spawning in while it was happening, something that basically no other game can say. It allowed me later, while playing the game for myself, to prepare for the next wave in a way I felt I had never been able to before. That is just one sound, and it completely shifted my perspective on the game.

It goes further than that with Hades, though. Different sounds are applied to a multitude of different things, kind of like the sweeteners we use in some audio cues. For instance, I can listen to someone playing Hades and determine what blessing they have on their dash, and even their attack and special abilities as well in some cases. I could also tell you which aspect most weapons in the game were currently using.. All this is because every single one of these little details is given its own individual sound that is layered upon the attack or dash or special move. When you dash with Athena's Divine Dash blessing, for instance, each dash is accompanied by a short, bright little sound. It's subtle, but it's enough to differentiate it from the other versions of dash, buffed or unbuffed. This attention to detail also applies to curses put upon your enemies from other boons. I can always tell when an enemy has been weakened, or afflicted with the Hangover curse, and so on.

There's more to truly accessible audio design than differentiating attacks or weapons. Sometimes it's about just including extra detail. Remember, audio designers, you are creating the version of your game world that we blind gamers will get immersed in. So, every single extra detail does matter. The sounds of your character sliding into tall grass, the sound of a fire we're supposed to escape from, and the new footstep sounds that play when we begin walking on unstable terrain. All this and a million other things matter to us. Let me give you a couple of examples.

I'm going to go back to old faithful here, The Last of Us. There is audio detail here that, if it hadn't been there, many probably wouldn't have noticed, but I sure noticed it existed. For example, did you know that, when looking through all the items in your backpack, each one plays a different sound as you pull it out and put it away? Notes make papery rustling sounds, Joel's watch in TLOU2 sounds like, well, a watch, the firefly pendants make little clinking sounds as you swap them. The list goes on.

Of course, swapping every weapon feels different, but what about putting them away? I was shocked when I noticed that, when you put away the flamethrower, you can hear the fuel canister clinking against either the flamethrower or the other items in your pack. It doesn't matter. It just matters that it's there. Our imaginations take care of the rest. Each weapon has a put away sound, of course, but the flame thrower is the most noticeable.

Then there's the detail I referenced in the previous chapter, where walking and crawling sounds also change depending on which weapon you're carrying. Crawling while holding onto a huge rifle is particularly loud. These details are truly fantastic, but it gets even better.

In The Last of Us, you can check the current status of your silenced pistol, but I almost never need to. I might check to make sure the silencer is equipped when I first pull out the pistol, but after that, I'll never check again because there is a distinct audio when your silencer pops off, becoming useless. But it gets better than that. The can uses as part of your silencer and then becomes an object in the world. One that you might accidentally kick aside as you keep moving. That little detail is so fantastic. That little canister would be the easiest thing to just delete, but that's not what happens, and it still stands out to me as an audio detail I appreciate immensely.

I think I've made my point here. In summary, fill your games with audio. I know there are already some incredible audio designers out there doing a great job now, but I even want them to take a listen to their work and look for those extra details they might be able to add. Surround us with different environmental audio. Get reverb and echoes as accurately as you can. Concentrate on making sure the audio position of every object is as accurate as possible. And then just start adding details. The smallest little things could spark imagination or provide a little bit of extra knowledge. Be as vigilant as the graphical artists, because again, it is you who makes our game world for us.

CHAPTER 15

Audio Description and Scripted Events

On the heels of our lengthy discussions on the power of audio and audio cues, we now move into yet another way to help immerse your players in your game world—audio description. In case you haven't heard of it before, audio description is an audio track overlayed over media that describes the visual elements of that media. It is often used in TV shows and is supported by the bigger streaming services today such as Netflix, Max, and Disney Plus. There is even live audio description, where a narrator often sits in a separate booth, watching the action, and broadcasting their descriptive narration to those in the crowd wearing headsets configured for that purpose. You might find this kind of description at a sporting event, a concert, a play, or lately, even a video game show like the Game Awards.

More recently than all these things, however, you will even find some audio description in video games. What am I going to mention next? That's right, you guessed it, The Last of Us. When we were working on TLOU1, the remake of the 2013 game, we worked with a well-known audio description company called Descriptive Video Works to add audio description to the cinematic moments in the game. This meant that, when you reached a cinematic scene, it would be accompanied by a narrator describing events in a succinct way. One of the goals of audio description is to not step on dialog or important sound effects, and this was done in the cinematics for

DOI: 10.1201/9781003433750-17

The Last of Us Part I as well, making them feel like the blind, like all the other media they consume with audio description. This was universally well-received, but there was a pretty significant drawback as well.

There is a reason I emphasized the fact that the audio description in TLOU1 was for the cinematic moments. It only applied to the prerendered cutscenes, but not to any scripted event that happened in-engine. As you may know, The Last of Us has a TON of these. The best example is part of the introductory sequence, where you're playing as the character Sarah, and are a passenger in your uncle's car for several minutes. Because of this implementation, this entire sequence is undescribed, up to the point where the running sequence that comes after it ends, at which point the game cuts to a prerendered cinematic. Still, as this was the first instance of audio description implementation of this type, the blind generally felt good about it.

There are a couple of games that took things a bit further. Forza Motorsport, for instance, has audio description that applies both to its pure cinematics and to some specific gameplay moments. As you start a race or practice, for example, you'll hear a bit of dynamic audio description that describes the weather and track condition while also telling you what's happening. As you enter the pit during a race, you'll hear a description of that, and if you make changes there, you'll hear a description of the swift actions your crew takes to make that change. This implementation of audio description brings us a little closer to the idea of what audio description in games could be in the future.

But it's not the only example. Mortal Kombat 1 contains audio description for its entire cinematic story but also includes it for its biggest moves, Fatal Blows and Fatalities. As these moves are triggered, audio description kicks in, describing the over-the-top violence of these moves. This is especially impressive during Fatal Blows, which are now double team moves between you and your assist character, or Kameo, as they are known in the game. The moves are split in half, and therefore so is the audio description. One character's action is described first, transitioning smoothly after into the actions of the second character. Even certain extra cinematic moments, such as the moment that plays when you defeat the final boss in the game's arcade mode, are audio described, giving those moments a little extra flare for the blind.

Mortal Kombat 1 does something else with its audio description too. During the story mode, there are specific moments where the player must complete a mini game to proceed. If you don't succeed at these mini games, the characters you're controlling at the time will die, often horribly, and you are forced to retry until you succeed. However, the important thing here is that audio description works in both scenarios. Yes, even the failure states are described, bringing a little bit of the dynamic into MK1's cinematic story description.

Another example of audio description in a game is Stories of Blossom, which has arguably the fullest and most in-depth audio description so far. However, this is largely because implementation in a game like this (a point-and-click adventure) is relatively simple, since the entire game is composed of selecting objects and then watching as an animation plays. Still, it was well done, describing rooms as you entered them, characters as you interacted with them, and events as they unfolded. Developer Softleaf Studios also took the interesting approach of pausing everything else in the game while audio description was playing, thus removing the time restriction that usually surrounds audio description. This may not always be the best approach, mind you, as you don't want to pull players out of an action-heavy sequence for too long, but for this game, it worked wonderfully.

There's another type of audio description used in 1428: Shadows Over Silesia. While it, too, describes its cinematic moments, it also has an on-demand audio description feature. Press a specific key, and the current room you're in will be audio-described. This is a great idea and may be ideal for some games where describing a room the second it is entered doesn't make sense. Consider whether events occur as rooms are entered, or if a room is entered during a cut scene, after which the player is given back control there. These might be situations where you should consider having a dedicated command to describe the player's environment.

So, what is the future of audio description, and how can you make it a part of your project? I'm so glad you asked. The way I see it, the future of audio description is dynamic. Every moment the user isn't in control could, and should be described, and I think that some moments where they are in control could also be described. For instance, if your game is one of those interactive movies like the Dark Pictures Anthology from Super Massive Games, why couldn't those running sequences be audio-described just like everything else? You're made to make decisions quickly in those, but as long as the quick time events themselves were also accessible, you could either audio describe each little split segment or, if necessary, due to incredibly small time windows, do a bit of a time slowdown or pause while the description of events was occurring. The description that played could be based on the game's preexisting knowledge of what would happen based on the player's choices so far, and if more time was needed to describe something than was available in the scene, you could insert something to make it clear time is being slowed or paused for this, (those bass-filled sounds for slow motion that movies have made popular for instance), and get your describing done before ramping back up into the action. If done right, you won't even lose the intensity of the moment because good audio description narrators keep up the tone of the action taking place. This would be complicated to code, but it would be worth it.

And speaking of worth it, if you do pursue audio description in your project, I highly encourage you to utilize an existing audio description company, such as the previously mentioned Descriptive Video Works, to handle the writing and recording of audio description for you. There are several reasons for this. Firstly, they are willing to negotiate. As much as I've seen the concerns about audio description being too expensive, I've heard from high-ranking folks in these companies directly that they are often willing to work out something fair. Second, they are professionals. The writers who write audio descriptions are specially trained to do so in such a way that they don't step on dialog yet still manage to communicate all the important visual elements of a scene. The narrators who do this professionally have mostly been doing it for years, and they know how to apply the proper tone to each scene. On top of that, many of them are recognizable.

This might come as a surprise to you, but the blind community recognizes their favorite audio description narrators in the same way that anyone who consumes movies, TV, or games might recognize their favorite actors. I have literally given certain shows a chance because one of my favorite narrators was narrating the audio description. A game that has one of our favorite narrators on it doing its audio description might just mean more than you know.

Just one more audio description tip. When you hire these companies, listen to them. I'm not saying you, the developer, shouldn't have some say in how things go or who the narrator is, but make it a conversation rather than a demand. Much like accessibility consultants, these audio description folks know what they're doing and are in the positions they're in for a reason as well. I think true collaboration is how you create the best product.

Also, I suppose I should address the elephant in the room, which is audio description done by text-to-speech instead of a human narrator. To that, I say this. If you can, please avoid the TTS audio description. A human narrator is far preferred for audio description, as they can inflect and create the proper amount of nuance and emphasis that makes audio description stand out. TTS just cannot do that. However, if there is some reason you cannot do a human-narrated description, be it for budgetary reasons or implementation issues or whatever, if the choice is to do a TTS audio description or have no description at all, then go ahead and do an audio description with TTS. We would much rather it exist than not. And the good news is professional audio description companies can still be utilized in this circumstance, as you can specifically hire their writers to write the description you will then use TTS to implement. Just know that, if you can spring for it, human narration is where it's at.

Audio description is yet another powerful tool in your arsenal that can help you make your game accessible to the blind. Describe your cinematics and in-engine cut scenes, give players a way to describe their environment, and even describe some interactive and scripted events, even if that starts with just describing both the success and failure states of an important quick-time event. You have examples of almost all these things in this chapter to refer to. Study them, and then help to craft the future of accessible gaming with audio description.

CHAPTER 16

Combat and Kombat

LET'S BE REAL HERE, lots and lots of games feature some sort of combat. Certainly not all games, in fact there is a lovely showcase dedicated exclusively to nonviolent games called the Wholesome Showcase, but still, many, many games feature some sort of combat. During this chapter, we're going to discuss how you could make those different types of combat accessible. There's so much to say on this subject, in fact, that this chapter is split into sections! NOW we're writing a book. Anyway, let's choose violence and begin walking the path to its accessibility.

16.1 ACTION/SHOOTER COMBAT

This first section is intended to cover the wider varieties of combat. I will do my best to cover as many types of combat as I can because there is a lot of ground to cover here. This section is called Action/Shooter combat, and I do realize that is underselling it, but just know this is what you want for MOST of your combat needs. Here we go.

Let's start with shooters. Shooters, especially very fast-paced, high-intensity ones like Call of Duty, are complicated, but they can work, possibly even in a multiplayer setting, though we'll discuss that in a later chapter. For now, let's focus on single-player, and what it would take to get a blind player through the combat in a Call of Duty-like story. To be clear, these ideas could apply to any shooter, be it Doom or Borderlands.

There are a couple of options when approaching the shooting in a game like this. The first is just pure, very raw aim assist. Snap to targets the second the player holds or presses the aim button, play some kind of cue to let

DOI: 10.1201/9781003433750-18

them know they have a target locked, and let them have at it. Now I know what some of you might be thinking, and I urge you to calm the shouting of your sighted person brain. You're thinking that's too easy, that it won't achieve what you want to achieve with the story. Well, if we were talking about multiplayer, I would agree. This method is too easy to be valid in multiplayer. However, games at their core should be fun, and I promise you, the blind are, in their heads, living that dream of being amazing shooters destroying their enemies, no matter how much the game is helping them do that. To put it in perspective, I'm going to do what I always do, and go back to The Last of Us, because yes, this IS the method we used for that game, and I promise you tons of blind people love it.

However, there is another method I've been cooking up for a while, and I would like to see this one applied to multiplayer, because I think it would be a good option. I would like to hold the aim button, and if there is a target in range, get a reticle sound that lets me know that it is played in the horizontal position of that target. Then, it is my responsibility to line up the sound so it's in the center, which will confirm I'm aiming at that target. If 3D audio gets better, I would suggest we could do this for the vertical targeting as well, but aiming at the horizontal spot, and having the game then help us with the vertical would be a good starting point, I think. Sea of Thieves did try something like this with its aim assist, using pitch to indicate the vertical position, and while I absolutely admit that technically works, it also seems too slow for a higher-paced game. To have it click in one spot but still have to find another would be difficult. Plus, the game may have to slightly account for distance as well. Still, I think this sort of system could work with enough tuning and testing.

Now, let's talk about taking cover. Having a player go invisible, like The Last of Us, is a potential solution but not an ideal one. The goal here is to preserve as much of the experience as possible while making a game accessible. The real cover system I envision would work like Gears of War's pretty brilliant system, which will run to a cover spot for you just by holding A and a direction. Of course, this would need to be accompanied by some additional audio cues to provide the player with some necessary information. For example, if no cover existed in the direction the player pressed, an audio cue should quickly alert them to that fact. Next, when cover is successfully found, and the character dashed to it, a cue should play to indicate the level of cover that has been achieved, be it half cover, full cover, and so on. If that cover is destructible, this cue should play again whenever the state of the cover changes, as it is getting destroyed. This will allow the player to decide as to when to leave that cover and dash to another one.

There are other things to consider when making the full experience of a shooter accessible, but we're specifically focused on combat here, so let's move on for now. What about action combat that may not involve guns? The quick sword-slashing of Diablo, or the free-flowing combat of Arkham City or Marvel's Spiderman? The first key to close-quarters stuff is to have some sort of enemy lock-on system. It is the lock-on system, along with a couple of other things, that makes the combat in Kingdom Hearts its only blind accessible feature. Locking onto a target influenced your movement, so locking on, then rolling forward, or executing a move that pushed you forward would send you toward your chosen target. This was an extremely helpful aspect of design, as it allowed me to locate enemies and bosses with ease. There is even one boss that must be hit by a thrown object before he can be damaged, and it was no problem to target the object, move toward it, pick it up, lock onto the boss, and just press the same button to throw it right at him. Whether intentional or not, Kingdom Hearts did it right.

Second, some helpful audio cues would be nice. You can use the enemy's existing audio for this, for the most part. Hearing a character obviously wind up an attack as a signal to dodge is fine, but there are a few questions to be considered here. Do your enemies execute each of their attacks with the same timing? Is the dodge window smaller than the windup window, and can the beginning of the actual swing be detected by audio? Also, are you planning on adding the ability to adjust dodge windows as an accessibility feature? Are there big, huge boss attacks that can be dodged but whose audio is very long and not obvious with its tells? Definitely a lot of questions here, but they're worth asking, because they might help you decide if you might want to add a dodge sound cue to your game. Just a sound that plays during the exact dodge window for each attack, allowing players to get the timing down.

The Last of Us went with both obvious audio tells for incoming attacks, and a dodge audio cue, and the bloater is a large part of the reason why. A bloater is big and slow, and its windups are long, so pressing the dodge button as soon as the windup starts isn't wise. You will probably dodge too early and get crushed for it. The dodge cue is a teaching tool that shows us at what point during that long windup to actually dodge. It's the kind of thing some might even turn off after a while, but it's very useful.

If your game has other things tied to its combat, such as a good reason to build a combo meter, or abilities that have cooldowns, it is important to identify these things as well with either narration or audio cues. Let players know when they can pull off that big super move, or when an ability they might want to use is ready. Giving each individual ability a different cooldown sound would be helpful as well, since a blind player who has learned the sounds of their abilities will instantly know which one is ready.

Let's move onto turn-based combat, which is probably the simplest thing to get working. If you're making a fairly conventional JRPG, all you need to do for combat is narrate the menus and provide status information such as health and effects applied or removed from each character as it happens. As long as we have all this information and can examine our party and our enemies so we can learn all there is to learn about them, we can succeed. And to be clear, we wouldn't ask for an unfair advantage either. Say your game is like Final Fantasy in that you don't see an enemy's health unless you use some sort of sensor or scan ability. Fine. Hide it from us as well until then.

If your combat is turn-based but incorporates things like movement, we will need ways to get significantly more information. We need some kind of free-moving look-around mode where, without affecting any character positions, we can examine the battlefield and receive cues for appropriate things depending on which exists in your game. Cover, or objectives that must be reached, or enemies, or hostages, whatever elements might exist on the battlefield need to be identifiable to us. We also need to be made aware of how enemies are moving on their turn so we can effectively move to counter them (again, keeping in mind that we aren't asking for more information than a sighted player would get at any given point), and any relevant updates to the battlefield. When making combat-related decisions, we need all relevant information. Chance of success of a shot in a game like XCOM, for example. Anything a sighted player would know, we need to know as well so we can make those same decisions. Also, situations where an action may affect multiple targets (even the little targeting click you hear in 13 Sentinels is helpful), information about those targets, and so on. This is the kind of system that would likely require much testing and iteration to get right, but I see no reason why it couldn't be done.

Speaking of strategy, let's briefly talk about RTS (Real-Time Strategy) combat, if only to say that the combat itself in an RTS game isn't usually the concern. We would need to receive regular information in regard to the combat, (integrity of our structures, life of our units, and so on), but playing an RTS for us is more about being able to quickly examine information and react to it, as well as have an accessible way to select and move units. Not much combat concern there.

What about a game that works something like Space Invaders? We can do that too. There are already audio-only examples of this, such as a game called Judgement Day, which is made by L-Works and is, unfortunately, abandonware, but to my knowledge, still works as of this writing. Essentially, every approaching enemy or ship is a positional sound source, and it becomes our job to move toward them until they are in the center of our stereo field. So, if our enemy is on the far left, we move left until they are centered, and blast them. This could be done in a similar video game too, I believe, though it may be necessary to incorporate game speed options as well. I'm not able to confirm this, but based on my experience, it seems to me that visual processing is still faster than auditory processing. Maybe I'm wrong. I would definitely love to hook up with a developer who is willing to try this experiment.

What about full-on air combat? I'm talking full 3D movement, swooping by to make a pass at your foes, that kind of thing? Well, it's complicated, and again, we're just talking single-player for now, but I think it can be done. Of course, we need some kind of lock on system so we can locate and approach our enemies. Much like Kingdom Hearts, our lock on should tie into navigation somewhat, helping us get within range of our targets if necessary. Incoming fire from our enemies could also have audio cues attached to them while traveling, enabling us to better attempt a dodge. Something similar could also apply when our enemy is locked onto us, allowing us to try to break it. It would have to be a carefully designed combination of sound and assistance, but it could work.

Let's head back to the ground for vehicle combat, like you'd find in Mario Kart. In cases like this, we would need to be much more aware of our environment, whether that was a track or a city street. For this reason, you might want to apply some of the principles from the racing chapter, which is later in this book. Other than that, the same ideas apply for vehicle combat as in air combat. Some kind of targeting system, which also ties into racing assistance navigation, might be needed, unless it is specifically a race that also includes vehicle combat, in which case we would just need to know enemies near us and focus on racing assistance to navigate the track. All weapon selections would need to be narrated, as well as powerups collected. And of course, the powerups themselves would need to be positional sound sources so we could locate and collect them. All the better to start blasting away at our friend.

16.2 KOMBAT: FIGHTING GAMES

Fighting games are an interesting breed. There is both a whole lot and very little to consider when approaching the blind accessibility of a fighting game. Out of the box, they are the most accessible genre, without a doubt. With very few exceptions (Marvel Nemesis being one of them), most fighting games always place you directly across from your opponent. There is, therefore, never any real question of where your opponent is. You always know that if you throw a fireball, it'll go toward your opponent. If you jump forward, assuming you know which direction forward currently is, you'll jump toward your opponent. Navigation isn't the issue here; it's everything else you have to worry about. Let's talk about how to make accessibility happen in a fighting game.

Fighting game accessibility starts with the things you may already be doing as a fighting game developer. When designing your audio, focus on uniqueness. Make every attack sound stand out as different from every other. Give every character a unique voice, so every grunt is easily identifiable. The Nickelodeon All-Star Brawl game didn't do this, giving characters no voices whatsoever, making it infamously impossible for a blind player to follow. Even attempting to listen to the game on a stream was a no go.

While you're over there making everything sound amazing, do consider the stereo field. It is a nice way to communicate player position. The way it should work is, if a player's audio is playing all the way off to the left, then they are on the far left. The same goes for the right. The listener's point should be approximately the center of the screen, so if both players are duking it out in the middle, their audio will be approximately centered. As one drives the other into the corner, both of their audios should move that way. You get the idea, but it's amazing to me that some fighting games today still do not do this. I'm looking at you, Tekken 8, with your thin stereo field that seems to only communicate vaguely which side a player is on, but nothing else. Most fighting games (Mortal Kombat 1, Street Fighter 6) are doing this right.

Those are the basics of the natural accessibility that fighting games possess. How do you take that further? Well, Mortal Kombat 1 and Street Fighter 6 will both tell you how. Those games have additional audio cues that provide even more information to a blind player, such as a cue that gives you the distance between opponents. This one may not be essential for experienced players, as they will become used to using the natural stereo field, but it is very useful for new players just learning the game, and for players working out the ranges of each attack. There are also cues that indicate the type of each hit, as in low, mid, high, and overhead. This is extremely useful for learning and adapting to your opponents, as well as studying your own characters so you know how to avoid or block each incoming attack and know where your own attacks will connect so you can create mix-ups.

Mortal Kombat 1 has even more audio cues for ducking and blocking, so you can tell when your opponent is doing one or both of these things and act accordingly. This levels the playing field further, as the sighted could see the block or duck animations.

Other audio cues might indicate the status of each player's health meter or super meter or break gauge or any gauges your game may have. These sounds usually play from that player's HUD side. So, if player one's health dropped to 20%, for instance, their health meter sound would play from the left. These things might seem hard to keep track of, but I promise you they're extremely useful in the moment.

Other than that, try applying narration to things that, in the past, the blind never had access to. Move lists, tutorial messages, anything a player could use to "lab" a character, should be narrated. All the practice menus, frame data, all that. Of course, this goes back to the narration chapter's philosophy of narrating everything. Every text element of any kind should be accessible to the blind in some way. This is just a specific example of giving the blind access to information they never used to have. I refer you again to Mortal Kombat 1, as though its narration isn't complete as of this writing, it does have these specific elements, prioritized for narration first because of their necessity.

And lastly, why not add some audio description in there where possible? Again, I refer you to Mortal Kombat 1, as nearly every cinematic moment is audio-described, from the opening cut scene to the entire story mode to all fatalities and the super moves known as Fatal Blows. There is a lot of potential for high-intensity audio description in fighting games. I even think Mortal Kombat 1 should add more. Who knows, maybe they have by the time you're reading this.

And that is combat accessibility. We've approached combat from quite a few angles, and I hope this has given you some idea of how to welcome the blind into the fight. Don't be surprised when we win.

CHAPTER 17

Puzzles

SOMETIMES YOU NEED A good puzzle. Something to keep the player's attention and make them think a little bit. Something that they feel good about completing when it's done. Puzzles can be a nice change of pace and create gameplay opportunities that wouldn't otherwise exist, but how do you make those puzzles accessible to the totally blind? That is what we're about to discuss in this chapter.

The first game that wasn't an audio game to really approach this question was The Last of Us Part II. Throughout that game, there were several moments that had you trying to figure out how to reach a certain area or provide power to a certain generator. All careful moments that were meant to be studied and solved. However, the approach taken for The Last of Us Part II and subsequently Part I for its puzzles was to specifically script the navigational assist to guide you through each one. If you entered a puzzle area in which you had to pick up a ladder, you would first be taken to the ladder and prompted to pick it up. Then you'd be taken to the spot to place it and prompted to put it down. After that, you'd be prompted to climb it. Then you'd be prompted to grab the rope on top, hold the aim button, and aim assist would automatically aim across the gap at the spot you were supposed to throw the rope. I'm sure you get it; I'm just making the point that the puzzles are entirely scripted. They aren't even puzzles for us; they are simply things we must do in order to proceed.

Believe it or not, though, I am not entirely against this method. I do think it isn't the ideal choice, but I understand the reasons any developer may choose to use it. If time, costs, or other factors prevent you from using

DOI: 10.1201/9781003433750-19

the other methods of puzzle accessibility I'm going to suggest below, then use this scripted method. Ultimately, when it comes down to it, the blind player just wants to experience the story you've created through gameplay. If puzzles must be handled this way to ensure a blind player can make it through that story, then so be it. I guarantee you we will forgive the use of this method if it means we get to enjoy your game fully. That said, let's discuss some other approaches you could take with blind-accessible puzzles.

A quick note on the skip puzzle option:

I recognize the necessity of making puzzles skippable to ensure the game is accessible for as many players as possible. There are several reasons to include a puzzle skip option, from accessibility for the cognitively impaired, to generally accounting for those folks who might only have time for a short gameplay session and need to get to a save point rather than figure out that puzzle. That said, my solutions will focus on creating accessible means by which to complete a puzzle, rather than skipping them. Speaking strictly for blind accessibility, I do not like puzzle skips. Missing out on a chunk of gameplay because that's the only way I could get through an area feels wrong to me. Plus, these days, puzzles are so heavily tied into the narrative of games that you might miss more than gameplay. I'm the kind of person who likes to hear every second of character banter, and if that is happening during a puzzle, I would hate to miss it. So yes, you should have a skip puzzle option for those who need it, but also, if you could, try to implement one of these methods so that we might complete these puzzles as well. Thanks!

The first method is the simplified puzzle method. This won't work in every game, but a couple of good examples are Brok the InvestiGator and 1428: Shadows Over Silesia. In Broke, a blind player can select all hotspots from a menu. However, a sighted player would also have to worry about moving to the correct areas first in some cases. Sometimes, for instance, you have to jump onto a platform or drop down into a different area to select something. This game's version of simplified puzzles made it so this was done automatically or wasn't required at all. It literally provided a simpler version of puzzles, but one that still required some puzzle solving. This way, the player would still get that sense of accomplishment for having figured something out, but wouldn't have to worry about some of the more complex aspects of making the solution work. You still must provide the player with all the information they need in order to solve the puzzle, which we'll talk about more in a second, but adding in some simplification may help make the puzzle a bit more accessible too.

All this applied in Shadows Over Silesia too, except that game required the player to move manually, and would present unique menus on interacting with puzzle items. For instance, one puzzle required you to jump and climb in a specific way, but if Simplified Puzzles was on, you would be prompted to select which way you'd like to climb from a menu, and that would be handled for you. You still had to figure out the correct order to climb properly, but the process would be made easier to accomplish for the blind this way.

The second method is to just go all out on giving the blind player as much information, and as many ways to interact with the puzzle area as possible. This takes a lot of thought about the puzzle you're creating, and a ton of consideration of what your blind players may be missing. I'm talking detailed audio descriptions for the entire puzzle area. Depending on the puzzle, these audio descriptions may have to be dynamic as aspects of the puzzle are changed by the player's actions. There may need to be audio cues specific to that puzzle to help the blind understand its state. And most of all, the blind will need a method to select, and interact with, every relevant puzzle item as they please. This means not taking them from item to item automatically as in the scripting method, it means providing them a way to choose which item they'd like to interact with and, if the puzzle area is particularly large, helping them navigate to their item of choice. Basically, each puzzle would have to be its own accessibility subproject as you gave the blind player as much information, and as many tools, as you could. This would, without question, be the toughest approach, but it would also be the most rewarding, as it implies the fewest actual changes to your puzzle.

The final method is to change the nature of the puzzle for your blind players, allowing them to solve a puzzle that still fits, but is made for them. This would be difficult to apply to puzzles that involve the level itself, such as moving objects onto panels to open a door in the level, (though again specific audio cues could be made to help with that), but could be applied to puzzles where the player interacts with one specific object to make something occur once that interaction is complete. Imagine the hacking puzzles in some games, or the science puzzles in all the Spiderman games. These are the kinds of puzzles that could benefit from this kind of treatment. Maybe for the blind, puzzles like this are audio puzzles that require you to, for example, make every note match, or achieve harmony with the adjustable notes you've been given. These are very basic examples, but I believe you get the idea. We're not going to be able to rewire circuits we can't see, but give us a puzzle based on what we can hear, and we've got this.

And those are my suggestions for making your puzzles accessible. Any one of them is OK, and it's possible that your game may require more than one. Honestly, I would love to see a game that classifies itself as a puzzle game, one that is essentially ALL puzzles, made fully blind accessible using these methods. One playable by both blind and sighted alike. But now, though, it's time to switch gears, and I mean that literally.

CHAPTER 18

Racing and Driving

A GAME THAT INVOLVES DRIVING brings with it a whole new set of challenges for blind accessibility, but certainly nothing we can't tackle. After all, this book is coming to you after I've helped launch Forza Motorsport, which is a simulation circuit racer with full blind accessibility. It can be done. Let's talk about how.

For a circuit racer like Forza, we focused on providing the blind with the information necessary to get around the track. Therefore, we added audio cues to give them an idea of where the edges of the track were, when they were heading into a turn, the sharpness and direction of that turn presented as racing coach voiceover, a deceleration cue to give them an idea of when they should slow down to start turning, turn gate cues to let them know when they were at the beginning, the apex, and the end of each turn, and a steering guide that panned their engine audio left or right to help them get the turn angles correct in real time. These features were backed up by a lookahead system, which was essentially there to account for player reaction time. Lookahead would literally lookahead of the player on the track, and the steering guide and deceleration cues would be connected to that, so the player could react to the sounds they were hearing. Moving the lookahead further meant you had more time to react, but did risk you reacting too early and thus turning too early, which can cause its own problems. Decreasing the number brought lookahead closer to your car, meaning you had less reaction time, which could ultimately improve lap times, but risked you reacting too late. The key was to find the

DOI: 10.1201/9781003433750-20

lookahead setting that worked for you, so you could react at the speed you needed to.

Of course, in introducing these features to blind players, we had to keep in mind that most have never driven a car before and may not even understand how actual car physics works. It was therefore important to provide as much onboarding as possible to teach players these basic concepts, since they were headed into a simulation game. Audio racing games did and do exist, (Top Speed 3, Rail Racer), but those games don't use real car and track physics the way Forza does, so it was important that players get a basic understanding of these concepts. For instance, in audio racing games, you typically don't have to slow down when you're making a turn. It's all about going at top speed and making your turns at the right time. Now, we had to learn to judge turns and figure out how much we had to slow down for each. Of course, the audio cues helped with this, but it's still a difficult concept to take in when you're not used to it. I had to learn it myself while working on the project, which I believe benefited our ability to present this, and other concepts to newer players.

But of course, there are other things to consider besides circuit racing. What about driving in a game that isn't a racing game? How does one approach that? Well, there are a couple of ways. First, there is the Watch Dogs' method. Allow the player to accessibly select a waypoint, then activate an auto drive mode which takes them directly to it. It is a viable solution and, depending on the game, may be accepted by the blind community. Of course, I will always advocate for full control, so let's talk about how that might be achieved.

First, let's talk about driving when there is a path for the player, be that a specific driving mission, or a situation where a blind player has selected a waypoint and has a set destination. In this case, you could choose to take some cues from Forza's blind driving assistance. If the player is driving on roads, you could call out upcoming turns along their path and provide them with steering guide assistance by panning their engine left or right to help them turn the correct amount. If they're not driving on roads, you may still be able to call out turns, though it will likely have to be more generalized and nonspecific. While on roads, you might be able to include turn sharpness in a similar way to what we did in Forza, this may be more difficult when driving to a destination out in the open. Still, even if you're sticking to "turn left" and "turn right" as ways to prepare the blind player for the upcoming turn, you can use engine panning to help them take the turn, the sharpness of that turn then indicated by the amount the audio pans, and how severely it does so. There will also have to be an indicator of when the blind player has driven past their turn (if they didn't turn enough, for example, and are now going the wrong way), as well as a way for them to relocate their path. This could be done with audio cues or with a dynamically updating steering guide system that will put them back on the path.

But what about when there's no path? What if the blind player chose to drive out in the open without setting a destination? Well then, your focus becomes object awareness, as well as awareness of potential hot spots of any kind. Some of these things, of course, can be used while driving with a destination in mind, such as traffic awareness while the player drives, where other vehicles might also be present. But when a player is truly out in the open, you may want to have audio cues for things they might encounter so they might drive around them. Trees, for instance. You may also want to indicate elevation changes, so they know if they're driving up a hill or mountain or descending a steep slope. And, if they are driving with no destination, you may want to have a specific audio cue that indicates where a road is if they're not currently on one. This way, if they feel like finding out what lies ahead that way, they can make the choice to drive onto the road while still having no set destination. Then, you use narration to indicate nearby points of interest, so if the player gets close enough to, say, a basecamp they can take over, they are informed and given the opportunity to make that their destination, at which point you revert to the previous rule set for getting them to that destination.

It wouldn't surprise me if the thought now in your head is that that's a lot of audio to process. I've just spoken about applying audio cues to a lot of things, and doing so in such a way that it can all be heard at speed. I promise, it doesn't have to be overwhelming at all, and probably won't be. The blind are capable of parsing quite a lot of audio. If you don't believe me, I recommend checking out the blind Forza community, because they are doing exactly that, and they are awesome at it.

CHAPTER 19

Open Worlds

OPEN WORLDS ARE POPULAR in games these days. Giving players the freedom to go wherever they like, do whatever they can imagine within your game's universe, is a powerful thing, and quite a draw for some. Breath of the Wild's notion that you really can just go straight to the final boss if you can find a way there is an intriguing idea. Not a recommended one, to be sure, but intriguing. But how do you give freedom like this to blind players? How do you make a massive open world, yet still manage to let them navigate and explore it? Can the sense of wonder still be preserved when the blind cannot see the incredible world you've created? We're going to discuss all those things in this chapter. Let's get to it.

19.1 NAVIGATION ON A WORLDLY SCALE

When talking about open-world navigation, we must break navigation down into two different categories. The first is the macro navigation category, where we're getting the player around the open world. For starters, this means a very smart navigational assist system. When the player has a destination, this system needs to get them there by not simply taking them as the crow flies, but by understanding the ways in which they can get there and helping them do so. If this kind of system were applied to, say, The Old Republic MMO, and my quest destination was on the other side of a planet, I would expect the navigational assist system to help me get there in one of two ways. If I activate my personal mount, then assume I want to use that and guide me on a path that will get me there. If I don't activate my mount, then guide me first to one of the in-game taxi services and help

DOI: 10.1201/9781003433750-21

me choose the appropriate destination that gets me closer to my ultimate goal by either placing an audio cue on the correct one or simply making the correct one the first to be highlighted in the destination menu. Once the ride is complete, keep guiding me until I've reached that destination.

And this leads me to my next point. Ideally, take control away from the player as little as possible. Nav assist should be done in a way that allows the player to make their own movements. The Last of Us' method, for instance, where they press a button to focus on their objective, but forward movement is still controlled entirely by them, is an acceptable solution here, even for long-distance navigation. It may be worth making nav assist a toggle, though, so the player isn't left pressing a button repeatedly for a very long time. And of course, in situations where the player wouldn't need to move their character, such as the taxy example we've just used, it's fine that control is lost. I specifically mean that any moment that a sighted player could control should be influenceable by the player.

I couldn't talk about this without mentioning Red Dead Redemption 2. They sort of got this concept half right. The cinematic camera approach, wherein you can press a button that activates a cinematic camera but also auto-navigates you to your set destination, is an interesting one. It only works while on a horse and is technically player-controlled as it has to be activated, but I don't like it's all or nothing approach. I understand this feature wasn't specifically designed for the blind, but if it was, why not let the player ride their horse but still guide them toward their destination? I don't like the idea of turning something you can control into a taxi, even if it gets you there. If I were to consider that approach for a project, it would absolutely be a last resort.

Let's step back a bit and talk about how the blind would set those destinations in the first place. The good news here is that the framework for the answer to this question is already built into most open-world games. You know that giant map with all those icons covering it, each one representing a different mission or activity of some kind? Yeah, that's the one. That is the framework you would use to get the blind to their chosen destination. The idea here is that we must make the map accessible to the blind in a way that makes sense, then attach the ability to set a waypoint on the map to the navigational assist path. So, how do we handle the map?

There is actually a very good reference for how to do a map correctly for the blind, and it's in a game that is otherwise inaccessible. Grand Theft Auto V, believe it or not, nailed the right idea here. In GTA V, you can press a button on the map screen, and it becomes a list instead, sorted by category of activity. This is how you do it. Don't ask the blind to move a free cursor around the actual map, even if it's narrated. It's still cumbersome, and inconvenient as, since we can't see the map, we're still likely to miss things available to us. Instead, allow the map to become a categorized, sortable, and of course narrated list, so we can choose the types of activities we want to do at any given time. If we want to do a side mission, let us sort by available side missions. If we want to take over a base, let us do that. If we want to go bowling because that's a thing you can do in this hypothetical accessible game, let us sort by bowling alleys. Then, once we've selected our chosen activity, drop a waypoint there and let navigational assistance help us get there.

Depending on the game, just doing these two things, making your map accessible and combining that with a smart navigational assist, could make your open-world navigation 90% accessible to the totally blind. Some particularly dense open-world games whose maps are just absolutely jam-packed with icons may be even closer to full navigational accessibility than that. But how do we make that 100%? We'll talk about that in the next section, but first, I want to go over just a couple more principles to keep in mind.

First, when making the map accessible, it's still OK to hide things from us. That might seem like an unnecessary statement to make, but I want to stress that I'm trying to help create parody of experience here. So, if your open world game only shows you some of the map at a time, the rest needing to be unlocked by, say, climbing to the top of a very high tower and looking out at the view, then only put what a sighted player would see on their map in our destination list. We want to feel the thrill of unlocking more activities and things to do as the game progresses, so hide what is meant to be hidden.

Second, it may be worth also considering allowing the list to be sorted and filtered in other ways besides activity as well. For example, distance. Maybe we're unsure of what we want to do, but we know we want to do something that's close to where we are now. Give us a way to show what is in our immediate area, and, when narrating the listed name for any activity, it might just be worth including the distance to it from our current position just so we have some idea of how long it'll take to get there, wherever it is. You could even include general cardinal direction in this narration as well, so if we wanted to, say, make our way toward a story mission that was far south of us, but also want to tackle a couple other side activities along the way that were also south of us, we could almost plot out a path from where we are now to each activity and finally to the mission. As I have said many times, it's all about information. Give us this information and ways to access all of it, and we've got this.

19.2 KEEPING WONDER AND EXPLORATION ALIVE

So, we've covered how to bring blind accessibility into about 90% of the open world. Now it's time to discuss how we get the rest to be accessible as well. Fortunately, I have some ideas for this. When exploring the real world, some people talk about how they just pick a direction and go. My idea for how one should start these exploration journeys is based on this concept. We're still going to need a little help, but there is a way we can pretty much do exactly this.

It all starts with an option to pathfind to the nearest unexplored area. You can base this on the direction the player is currently facing, so when this option is selected, the nearest unexplored area to them in that general direction will be selected. Then, they can use navigational assistance until they reach it. This should, of course, also present them with an error if there is nothing unexplored generally within that direction or if there might be, but it's currently unreachable. Again, it's OK to prevent blind players from reaching areas the sighted could not. This will effectively allow the blind player to pick a direction and go.

To be clear, the reason I am still advocating for the use of pathfinding in this situation (Why couldn't they just literally start moving in a direction to find new things?), is because being blind, we still do not know what is between us and the new area we're trying to reach. Navigating as the crow flies may not work in a world filled with stuff. I could just pick a direction and start moving, but what if I fell off a ledge, or hit a wall? Even if I found a way past the wall, maybe I'm now facing a different direction because it's difficult to track where you are at any given time in games like this. Even if the game supported audio cue-based navigational assistance, that may not account for the vast open space between where we are and where we want to be. And so, I believe pathfinding is still the best approach, even for reaching a generally new area.

Once we reach the new area, we'll still need to do the blind equivalent of looking around. This is why you will still need some kind of local scan, so we can get some lists or notifications, via audio cues or narration, of what's around us that we might be interested in looking at. Consider it a sort of mini map for the blind. We should then be able to select something nearby, and again, navigate to it with whatever assistance exists in the game. That will bring our ability to move through an open world game to probably about 95%. So no, we're still not done just yet.

To cover the last little bits of navigating an open world, we need some kind of informational notification when something that might be interesting is nearby. This could come with vague descriptions as well. Take Red Dead Redemption 2, for example. That game was very good at showing you interesting side quests while you were on the way from one place to another. You'd be riding somewhere and suddenly "Oh, what's that house doing all the way out here?" or "Who is that person just writhing on the ground like that, seemingly in pain?" Making this kind of moment accessible is the last piece of the puzzle. This is also the primary reason we always need to be in control of any kind of navigation, so that we might stop and choose to track this new thing we just found.

Of course, how much information you give to the player is entirely up to you. If you want them to have a shot at finding something neat when they get close enough, but don't want to tell them what it is until they find it, then don't. It would be very intriguing to sometimes get detailed descriptions of something we might want to go look at, but other times just be told that there's "something interesting" nearby, possibly with a mysterious audio cue accompanying that notification. Imagine traveling over land, then being notified there's something interesting nearby. Deciding we don't have to head to our story mission just yet, we choose to investigate and track it. After some movement, we find ourselves jumping into the water. "Whoa! I wonder what this is!" We end up diving, and then perhaps some audio description triggers, informing us that we have proceeded into an ancient shipwreck. We then proceed to explore using local scanning methods and possibly find some amazing new magical item or something. And all because we were told, at first in vague terms, that there was something interesting. I think that idea is very powerful. The notification intrigues us, then the ways in which the audio changes as we proceed give us that sense of wonder and finding something secret, and then the big reveal using audio description would seal the deal.

So that's it. That's how you make it so that even the blind can navigate a huge open-world game. I personally love the idea behind open worlds, so I find myself hoping that more developers will read this chapter than almost any other, but that's just me. Next up, one of the most difficult but necessary discussions in all accessible gaming—multiplayer.

CHAPTER 20

The Multiplayer Discussion

What follows is one of the most difficult discussions in accessible gaming—the question of how to handle multiplayer in video games, but maintain accessibility for the disabled. This discussion is especially difficult for the blind, whose needs are often many to make a game accessible in the first place. In this chapter, I'll attempt to tackle all facets of this discussion. The goal here isn't necessarily to provide a definitive answer (I believe this discussion will remain ongoing even after blind accessibility is more widely implemented), but hopefully it gets people thinking about all this, and maybe starts us down the right path toward working this out.

First, I want to address the most common arguments surrounding multiplayer accessibility, starting with the classic "Why should we do it at all?" Say a game has a single-player component, like a full campaign, and that campaign has been made fully accessible to the blind. Shouldn't that be enough? Why waste time trying to delve into this very difficult problem when we made single-player work beautifully? There is of course a lot I could say to answer that, starting with the obvious "Why not?" The most basic of questions regarding accessibility, since accessibility is absolutely the right thing to do. Why not include the disabled in every mode of your game? And that brings me to my next point.

The second answer would be because you cannot call your accessibility efforts complete until all modes of your game are accessible. A game

DOI: 10.1201/9781003433750-22

that claims something like, "Well everything works except for this," isn't a fully accessible game, and attempting to market it as such will just make disabled gamers angry. That, to me, is enough of a reason to consider trying to solve the multiplayer problem for your game. Being able to put the stamp of total accessibility on your game is going to feel good for you and look good for everyone else.

Next, I want to talk about another idea that has come up during this discussion. The developer who says "OK, we'll do it, but we'll put our accessibility features behind a specific flag and separate those with that flag from those who don't have it." I cannot dismiss this idea outright, much as I would like to. I would like to officially discourage you from doing this, simply because the blind or disabled may want to play with their abled friends, or even abled randoms. Putting them in separate lobbies will absolutely thin the pool of eligible randos, potentially leaving lobbies unfilled in certain high-capacity games. There are most likely more disabled people out there than some developers think, but still, the ratio of disabled players to abled is much smaller. It might be difficult to fill a Battle Royale lobby, for instance, with a segregated player base.

However, as I said, I can't completely dismiss the idea. Multiplayer accessibility is absolutely a difficult problem to solve, and I have enough respect for developers to acknowledge that. There are ways in which one might approach making multiplayer fully accessible and maintaining access for the sighted, which we'll discuss later, but if some of these things aren't possible in your game, or if you still don't feel the playing field is leveled and there is just no other way, then I would rather have a way to play multiplayer than not have one at all. Still, I strongly encourage you to consider this a last resort.

So, let's talk about implementation. How do we make multiplayer accessible without angering those who think adding accessibility features will just make things too easy, or having the abled use these features themselves to give them an even bigger advantage? This is where things get really complicated. The answer depends very much on the game, much as all accessibility does, but I'll give you a couple of scenarios that I've either talked about before or considered, the hope being that in doing so, you can start considering how to balance your game to make this work.

We'll start by going from extreme to extreme. Games like Mortal Kombat, for instance, don't really need any special modification to balance out multiplayer. As I've said in a previous chapter, fighting games are the most naturally accessible genre out of the box, and in general haven't required much accessibility modification, aside from narration and some informational audio cues, as demonstrated in Mortal Kombat 1. Because of this, the blind already have more than enough information to play Mortal Kombat online, and many have been quite successful at this. Blind players have even represented the community at major fighting game tournaments like Evo, leaving no doubt that we are on a level playing field there. Street Fighter VI, as well, has proven to be just as accessible, as a blind player, who recently competed on a professional level in that game as well.

But what about the other extreme? I have spoken to at least one developer about the idea that, if blind accessibility features are enabled, graphics are essentially turned off. That way, if the sighted turn on blind accessibility features, thinking they will just give themselves even more of an advantage, they will have to use them in the same way as we do, thus leveling the playing field in the reverse way. Again, I will say that I don't hate this idea. I think it's an interesting solution to the problem and wouldn't be surprised if someone tried this at some point. The problem, though, is that blindness is a spectrum, and those who have low vision may wish to use some of the accessibility features that would be in the list of features that disable graphics. Low vision users use narration, navigational assistance, aim assistance, and so on, all the time in games because, though they can see some, using these features allows them to work their eyes less, making the game less stressful and allowing them to act more quickly. So, it is a bit of a rocky road, which would likely get some pushback either way. Still, it's interesting enough that I want to acknowledge it as an option.

In terms of existing implementation, I want to talk a little bit more about Forza. The Forza team would be the first to tell you that, at least as of this writing, we don't feel our blind driving assist systems are well-optimized for the blind, and we want to do more. For instance, we don't feel our traffic awareness is up to par, which is a necessity when dealing with the unpredictability of actual players instead of AI opponents. However, we do still have a lot of confidence in our systems, confidence which I am happy to say has been rewarded, and so we simply chose to be honest about this. We informed the blind community of the potential struggles they might face in multiplayer but also reassured them that we wouldn't lock them out of it, which we haven't. Given that much of what we do in Forza is informational (narration and audio guidance around the track), it is still technically possible for a blind person to succeed in a multiplayer event despite these struggles, and some have. All our assists are allowed in multiplayer, with the single exception of events specifically set up not to allow them. Event settings can be previewed when joining, though, so that enables the blind to not participate in events that don't allow the settings they need. Also, we've committed to not disallowing these assists in any of the studio-created events, allowing the blind to try their hand at all the featured multiplayer events we can come up with. This appears to be a workable solution, and one that only gets better as our systems do, but it is also specific to our situation. Our audio cues and steering guide are enough of a navigational assist for the blind player, and they simply follow the same racing line that the sighted would be following. Again, different games may need different considerations.

In the chapter about combat, I discussed an aiming mode for shooters wherein the blind are required to manually center their target in their stereo field before any kind of aim assist would kick in, possibly helping them with vertical aiming if needed. This system could use a targeting indicator audio cue as well, using pitch to inform the player when they have a lock. When I spoke of that aiming system, I was thinking of multiplayer shooters. The sighted will never accept the blind having the same levels of aim assist we use in single-player games that have shooting elements like The Last of Us. It's too good. Too perfect, even. So, to make shooters more fair, a system that requires the blind to do some of the work is needed. There must also be a full cover system that uses audio indicators for cover and navigational assistance, specifically to allies or important items. All of these features will need to be carefully balanced of course, and tons of testing would be required, but I think the key here is to find ways to prompt the blind to do a bit more of the work than they may have to in single player (or just design all of your systems around these ideas so the difficulty is the same across the board), and try to balance that for everyone. Designing the game with accessibility in mind from the beginning is a must here, as it will better enable you to iterate, test, and balance for both blind and sighted players.

And so, as I said at the beginning of this chapter, there is no definitive final answer here. The approach to making multiplayer fair and balanced to all will have to be discussed at length for every multiplayer game, but one last time, I urge you to try. The blind don't want to be left out. They don't want to be told they can play one mode, but not the rest. They want to be a part of the game, and the conversation, just like everyone else. So, discuss it, and maybe give multiplayer accessibility a shot.

CHAPTER 21

Unexplored Territory

On one hand, there's no denying that accessibility in games has come a long way. On the other, there's a much longer way to go. The number of games that aren't specifically audio games and can truly be called totally blind accessible is still very small. Games like The Last of Us, Forza Motorsport, Sequence Storm, and As Dusk Falls are incredible, but there is still so much territory that is yet unexplored when it comes to blind accessibility.

What about platformers, for instance? What about Mario or Sonic? That's the territory we should explore. I think it would be such fun to truly be able to experience the star-collecting, level-completing, and even secret-finding of a Mario game. To do this, you might combine some of the principles we've discussed here. Navigational assist so we know which way we're supposed to go, but less traversal assistance, and more reliance on audio cues and perhaps haptics to communicate the information we need to know about the obstacles in our way. Give us a sort of camera mode that allows us to look around without committing to movement as well, so we could better learn about our environment. We may begin by going through levels very slowly so we can feel how the systems and cues work, but eventually, I believe we could take some levels at speed, and when we did, it would be a blast.

But what about giant 300-hour RPGs like The Witcher 3 and Skyrim? Yeah, we don't have one of those yet either. Imagine using some of the techniques I described in the Open World chapter to build something like that. A fully accessible, fully explorable world that we can just get lost in

DOI: 10.1201/9781003433750-23

for weeks. If a developer ever did that, they would be making many dreams come true, not just mine. Narrated quest logs, hundreds of pages of lore all narrated, an accessible map that we can sort by active quests or incomplete quests or known places, and so on. The possibilities are there; someone just needs to execute them. It's probably clear that this one's pretty high on my personal bucket list. I love deep narratives.

And speaking of deep narratives, how about walking simulators? Some of those games have compelling stories that have moved me, and yet I can't play any of them. Some light movement, some light puzzles, and some deep story sounds like a blast to me, and it would be relatively simple to enfold in the ideas I have presented here. Nav assist, puzzle modifications for audio, audio cues for different types of interactions, and narrated menus and text elements (notes, diary entries, and so on), and you'd probably be done. This is a genre I feel could work extremely well for the blind community.

There are unexplored aspects of the interactive movie genre as well. I'm thinking of companies like Super Massive Games when I say this. While As Dusk Falls was made accessible relatively easily since their scope was specifically limited to choices and quick time events, the Super Massive Games, such as the Quarry, have a bit larger of a scope. But in order to make it work, you simply combine the things that make As Dusk Falls work, (narrated menus and in-game text elements such as text messages, narrated quick time event commands, narrated conversational choices), with what you would need to make a walking simulator work, (navigational assistance, narrated browsable text elements such as collected clues), and then maybe you include some audio description as well to fully immerse the blind player. At last, we could make the choices that lead to the survival, or lack thereof, of these characters.

There are, of course, many other examples. I basically covered the puzzle games genre, another genre we don't yet have access to, in the chapter about puzzles. The multiplayer chapter is almost entirely about uncovered ground, hence the reason for all the uncertainty in that discussion. There is a lot of experimentation to do, and a lot of genres to open, and as this chapter demonstrates, you can often use combined examples from preexisting games or ideas for how other genres could be made accessible in creative ways on your own projects. Don't be afraid to innovate and iterate on these ideas to make them work for you, but also don't forget to work with consultants. I promise it'll be worth it.

CHAPTER 22

Conclusion

That's it, you've done it. You've finished the book. Either you read the entire thing, which I really, really appreciate, or you stuck specifically to the parts of the book that pertain to the project you're working on or have planned, which is fine too. No matter how you approached it, I truly hope you learned a lot about gaming from a total blindness perspective, and of course, how to approach blind game accessibility in your own work. We've covered a lot of ground here, so now I want to take a second to go over some final takeaways.

First, the usual suspects. Start thinking about accessibility early, design with accessibility in mind from the beginning, and of course, hire consultants. While it is my hope that this book was a great resource for you, there's nothing like having a consultant for each disability you're making your game accessible for to provide you with the perspective and insight, and later testing, you need to make it the best it can be. Also, accessibility is important, and there's no real reason not to do it. You want players to play your games, and making them accessible just means that more of them can.

Then, the takeaways for blind accessibility. First, when you break it down, it's all about information. Consider your game, consider what information your eyes provide you when you look at it, and consider that that's the information every blind player is missing. Then, find a way to either give them that information, or work around the fact that they don't have it, such as in the case of navigational assistance. And remember, ideas like the ones presented in this book might work for multiple genres or game

DOI: 10.1201/9781003433750-24

types, so don't be afraid to be innovative and combine them if that works for you. While you're doing that, though, preserve your own vision. As a consultant, I am not out to change the vision of the developer, I am out to make the specific experience they're trying to create more accessible. If a game is difficult, then the game should remain difficult. If a game relies on a certain moment feeling a certain way, one should try to preserve that feeling. (See my idea for how swinging through New York as Spiderman accessibly should work). Remember, we're going for as close to parody of experience as possible, just an accessible version of that.

And lastly, remember that we are gamers too, and we want to play your games. Look back at the history of gaming for blind gamers. Look at all the tenacity involved, the struggles we voluntarily went through to play games that weren't designed for us. The audio games were made to directly parody other games because those games weren't accessible. We are passionate about games, and we will reward your efforts to make them accessible with our loyalty, and our gratitude. We want to be a part of what you create. We want to join the game, and the conversation, right along with our sighted and otherwise able friends and our disabled ones too. Whether that's figuring out multiplayer or presenting us with an unforgettable narrative experience, we want in. Thank you for all of your work, but thank you most of all for reading this book and taking its contents seriously.

Index

For Product Safety Concerns and Information please contact our EU representative GPSR@taylorandfrancis.com Taylor & Francis Verlag GmbH, Kaufingerstraße 24, 80331 München, Germany

Printed and bound by CPI Group (UK) Ltd, Croydon, CR0 4YY
09/09/2025
01953122-0002